Wave of Blood

Ariana Reines
Wave of Blood

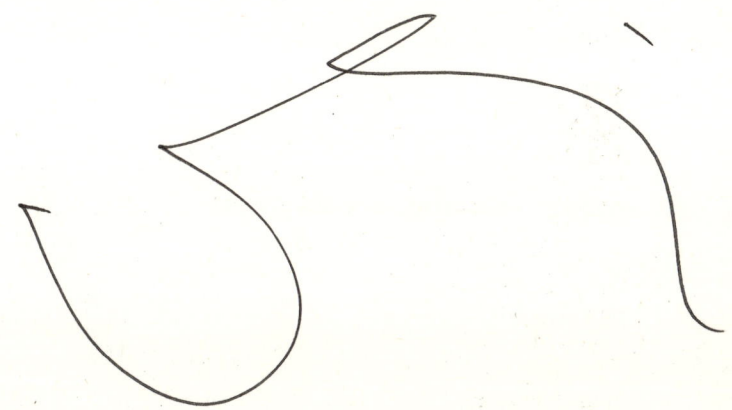

DIVIDED

Published in the United Kingdom by Divided in 2024.

Divided Publishing
Rue de Manchesterstraat 5
1080 Brussels
Belgium

Divided Publishing
Deborah House
Retreat Place
London E9 6RJ
United Kingdom

https://divided.online

Copyright © Ariana Reines 2024

All rights reserved. No part of this book may be reproduced or transmitted by any means without prior permission of the publisher.

Cover photo by Richard Joon Yoo
Designed by Alex Walker
Printed by Printon, Tallinn

ISBN 978-1-7395161-4-7

"Science must not replace pain, because when that kind of a catastrophe happens, it has no mercy."
—Etel Adnan, *Premonition*

A tortured soul can have social value—within certain structures and limits. Including temporal limits.

Suffering in a state of lucidity, you can draw out the repression and compacted pain in others.

But you must be careful not to go overboard.

And you must carefully demarcate the field of action.

Because every form of pollution can enter the procedure, from every direction, at and from every point in time.

It is like performing field surgery. You know the environment is nonsterile. Nevertheless the work must be done.

It is like performing field surgery on yourself. Suppose no physician were available or qualified to operate on a case like yours? Suppose no physician existed with such qualifications?

Such an act would test—overwhelm—your capacities, especially in the tricky parts, where you must navigate in spite of your inner weakness and general lack of perspective on the overall dynamic.

Operating theaters are pedagogical spaces.

Language, in spite of its corruptions, can reach places in the soul and body that heretofore only the obscurity of the ages—and prayer—could reach.

How do you transmute history?

How do you heal the suffering of your mother?

You must do everything possible and *also* everything impossible.

How else can this be accomplished but by incantation?

If you refuse to feel, your writing will die.

If you lie, get used to lying, the power in words will drain away.

Language, so long divorced from medicine, must snake its way back in.

How long does a soul last?

How much space does it occupy?

Begin now.

And continue to begin. When you grow weak, ask for help.

Then resume your work.

ABSOLUTE ZERO

To have seen
What I saw
Only yesterday
You would beg for God
As my heart did
Though it knew better
Kneeling and folded in on itself
Circumcised eye
Mouth hymning a tonsure
I saw a crimson hole
In the delicate skull of a baby
Going gray in the arms of her rescuer
Who prayed over her to himself
I would see God
Not this world we made
In its image
I would God saw what I saw
Not through me
But on my behalf
Not through me
But as my advocate
Lucre & bullion
The orbs of Milton
& Galilee
The lenses of Spinoza & Buchner
The sunsets of Borges
The suns of Stevie Wonder
And al-Ma'arrī, Santa Lucia's grave escape
Beauty was in the eye of the beholder

What I saw I did not know how to see
God almighty if there is a God
You must see it for me

I'm bleeding. I don't know why whenever anything important or difficult is happening this seems to be the case. Too much meaning for words—the rest pours out of my body.

The sense flooding me that I have to find a way to give myself absolutely to this world.

It's what the blood feels like and it's the feeling the writing comes from.

Or, it's how I give life.

As I write these words I can hear NYPD helicopters flying to and from NYU, where some faculty have joined their students protesting the genocide.

To sit here in language and blood is strange.

The moon will be full tomorrow.

Sometimes still I imagine raising children.

In the end I always wind up putting everything into writing.

This voluptuous, overwhelming dread and love—
I'm scared to leave it alone with nature. I press it into language.

But it's impossible—you can't fit all of life into words.

Especially bliss and love—the hardest things of all to tell.

I wrote this book to purge myself of suffering and to document a period of time.

To be precise, my intention was to document the period between the Libra and Aries Eclipses: October 2023 to April 2024.

The day after my birthday in October 2023 I went to Europe for a two-week reading tour. There was no financial reason to go. I had no new book to sell. But it had been arranged for me and had sort of set itself up naturally. I felt a Yes from God about it. That Yes had come before the war.

But there was always a war—already a war—before the war.

I didn't sleep all of October.

Or November. Or December.

What gave my life shape and meaning during this time was teaching Milton's *Paradise Lost* in Invisible College, a study hall for poetry and sacred texts I'd set up during the pandemic, while I was a Divinity student.

Studying *Paradise Lost*, and at night, when I couldn't sleep, reading Ecclesiastes aloud.

It may be that every true poem in fact opens the space of the miraculous—and keeps it open. Forever.

If I were honest I'd say: I started Invisible College because I wanted to study miracles.

By the time the book you are holding ends, I am preparing to teach another epic poem. But more about that later.

The reading tour surprised me. The last thing I wanted to do at that time was stand in front of people and read poems to them. I was in torment over the slaughter in Gaza, but also over Israel, where I have never set foot, and over my mother's death and the feeling my family line was dying.

Watching families killed and dismembered, little children. Things I had never seen. None of us. Unbearable things that magnetized me.

I was completely glued to my phone, as was everyone else I knew and loved.

I could not sleep, I was passing through the dark cities of Europe. It was cold and rainy everywhere but Lisbon. Everywhere the graffiti said Free Palestine. Everywhere in the world, my grandmother and my mother were dead.

This is part of the work of poetry or maybe it *is* the work—

You show up with what is in you and you tell it. There is no hiding from your heart. It is front and center. There is no hiding the you from you: The poems give form—and formality—to your grief and rage, to the grief and rage in the room.

To the shape of your love, and its depth.

What follows is poems and prose that I wrote during this six-month period, and also some public speaking that I did—almost without realizing it—during this time.

Marguerite Duras wrote that she did not remember having kept a notebook during WW2—but the notebook she did keep has been very important to me, and gave me courage when I was a young woman overwhelmed with despair.

I have told you the span of time this book covers.
I should also let you know it is *loosely* chronological.

The first poem that appears in this book, "ABSOLUTE ZERO," was the first poem I wrote during this period; my hated father's birthday preceded it. All time is circular, or spirals—as I know you know—or shall we say for the purposes of our time together here: It flows in waves.

Mostly, if you read on, you will see and hear a woman wrestling with the mind of war—in private, in public, and with a group of people with whom a sense of shared intimacy and care earned from years of study together makes possible a warm way of thinking.

My decision to volunteer my consciousness from this particular interval of time was initially a simple one—Freud says the recent past is the most difficult time for a person to recollect. I thought it would be a worthy exertion therefore, to face and sort through the particular anguish of the recent past—which is also the present.

I have left out of this book many other kinds of writing and speaking I also did during this period, and many things I struggled over in my notebook but could never resolve—places my mind and ethics collapsed, tormented and circular logic, regions of myself laid bare by horror that I neither knew how to soothe nor to educate.

"as if love/ could invent intelligence enough to save love—"*

---

*   From Sara Miles's poem "And Not Surrender," from the anthology *We Begin Here: Poems for Palestine and Lebanon*, edited by Kamal Boullata and Kathy Engel, published in 2007 by Interlink Books—posted recently on Instagram by Omar Berrada.

October 9, 2023—Invisible College

This time is—how can I say it—it's coming for all of us. It doesn't matter what side we are on, what kind of stories we're carrying, there's an agonistic and a heavy-duty quality to this autumn, it's bigger than me and it's bigger than you . . .

My father's birthday was last week, and I have carried enormous rage against this man in my body—my whole life. I'm not about to say that I forgave him because I don't know that I can.

For those of you who are new to this space, or new to me, some boilerplate: My mom became homeless when I was nineteen, and that's when she became my and my brother's responsibility. And my dad entirely turned his back on her, so did the whole family, such that my brother and I had to live out the consequences of her illness and abandonment alone and take responsibility for it alone.

It was the worst thing that ever happened to me. We never managed to create, not for lack of trying, but we never managed to create a kind of mutual aid or community of care to help us with her over the years. We just couldn't figure out how. I tried to set things up with the family but they just didn't understand, honestly, why what was happening to our mother mattered so much to us—how it was hurting us—what it felt like to be left alone with it.

We couldn't make them understand how much it hurt us—what was happening to her—and we couldn't make the rest of the family care—about what it was doing to her, what it was doing to us.

It wasn't until I started crowdfunding for her—once that strange new form of social media coincided with her eviction—that something like a community of support, where people weren't overburdened, somehow started to emerge. I never would have thought that the experience of crowdfunding could also teach my brother and me in this shocking yet gentle way that we were not as alone in the world as our family experience had taught us to feel.

I've given up my home multiple times through the course of my career, beginning when I was twenty. I've really given up everything, more than once. I've given up everything in order to have the privilege of being a "leftist" poet in this hypocritical society of ours. And I was really angry at my dad, I've always been incredibly angry at him. It has affected all of my relationships, all my romantic relationships, it's affected my relation to my entire family, to my tradition, to my religion, to my culture.

Though it's made me who I am. So on the one hand, I'm grateful. And I accept that this has been my path. But it's also been immensely agonizing and painful and lonely and shaming and othering and I had to basically watch my mother die for twenty years, and you know that will do something to a person.

This year on my father's birthday, I found a way to acknowledge him. I sent him a gift, which I've never done in my entire adult life.

In spite of all the ways that he has disappointed and hurt me, I found a way to acknowledge the reality that he is my father, and to do so with dignity. To acknowledge a fact. To face him, and say, You were the only father in this world for me. To finally accept and acknowledge that I am indeed his daughter, even though we have disavowed each other, been disavowing each other, for decades. So many things about him have horrified and disgusted me. Disappointed me. Made me sick.

I know from my studies in literature, ancient texts, I know from my pursuit, that all evil in this world comes from the same stuff. There's not some alien evil on this planet. When we see what we feel is evil, we're all made of the same stuff. And there's just no moving forward without a deep, deep introspection, and then a commitment to do what you can do.

So: I like many people have suffered. I have felt powerless, overwhelmed by despair—by the sense that evil is everywhere.

But to ruminate in this way makes me even angrier, and my thoughts become even more perverse. I've lived with shame—

That I could not save my mother, that I was born into a

family like this, that I felt guilty about it my whole life, that in some way I accepted to carry a curse and even volunteered for it—that I was willing to suffer like this. That I felt like this was what I had to do—suffer, and become an artist. When—who knows?

Where did I form this idea, or how did I form *in* it?

I've lived with the shame of what my direct family suffered. It's a twisty thing. These are all very twisty things, the evils that we endure, and the evils that we inflict. They are subtle, and they are gross. By gross, I mean big—there's the obvious loud ways that these things work. And they also engrave themselves within, somehow, and we can't always see everything, we can do wrong and act wrong and think wrong without realizing it. But when we do realize it, we have a duty to try and do something, and in the same way I realized on my dad's birthday, I felt this strangeness in my gut in the afternoon and I realized, Oh shit, I have to address this. I have to address this.

My rejection of him, his rejection of me—I can't live like this anymore.

I think there is magic in facing reality and acknowledging it. Many things that I hate are real. Saying they should not exist or pretending that they do not—somehow this dynamic seems to magnify the loggerheads, the evil. To say "I see you" to what most hurts me—I felt like: There's power there.

It's such a lonely feeling, to be treated beneath contempt. I created an identity and a life for myself, where I was able to renounce the natural desire to please my parent. I suppressed and repressed the desire to love my father and to be loved by him. I could start crying.

People often throw up their hands—they say, There's nothing I can do. And there's times when that is really true. That's real, there are times when that's really honest. But I've noticed as I try to become more rigorous and more precise, with my studies, with my actions, with my word, with my thinking, and by no means do I have it figured out, I realized when you *can* do something, it's important to do that thing.

I couldn't force myself to forgive my father—but I could acknowledge him.

I can't control how he behaves. I will probably never be satisfied with anything he may ever say or do.

He refused to come to my mother's funeral. Maybe the guy is a scumbag. And he is my father.

We human beings have so much disgust and revulsion and loathing of certain parts of ourselves. It is always what has torn and it is always what will tear the world apart. It was almost like a being rose up from my guts and was like, I know how you can acknowledge your father's birth and existence without compromising your dignity, without pretending that everything's fine.

But that will still allow you—me—to change, to transmute the moment, and I did it. I cried so much. I was so scared to do it. And I did it . . . I sent him a book I learned my mother had studied only at the mouth of her grave. And he thanked me for it and then I got angry, because his bland words of thanks seemed to erase the colossal inner effort I had made to make a gesture of love toward him.

And then I realized that it may be I will not be able to forgive him in this lifetime, and that one cannot do everything on one's own.

I will leave you with this. I've noticed, from watching myself, that what I hold on to maybe more jealously, what I guard more ferociously than almost anything else, at least up to this moment, has been my pain and suffering.

These things—pain and suffering—are defining, profound teachers. They cut into us so deeply. They engrave us. It's very, very hard to release. It's especially hard to do it when you feel like no one's cheering you on.

For me, doing that, acknowledging his birthday, was more important than anything that I could ever get a public accolade for. It was a ceremony of a great magnitude in my life. And it took my whole life and everything I've ever done to be able to do it, and it was deeply, deeply terrifying.

And, you know, that piece of shit doesn't deserve it right? But I needed it. Am I claiming that I've forgiven him?

No. But I can tell you that things are changing inside me because I did this, even though forgiveness is not in me as I speak these words.

In the arts we still proceed—in spite of our edginess—without questioning a lot of really old, dead paradigms. A lot of our older masterworks were made by miserable people who were completely delirious on a ton of drugs or sexually using people, I'm not trying to be puritan here about that. But I do believe art is awakening, just as we are living in an awakening universe.

Some of the pablum we have swallowed—whether that all geniuses are monsters or that all artists must be paragons of virtue—it seems to neglect that the terms themselves of what makes art great are shifting. We are actively part of this shifting; working at the edge of it.

I don't know what that edge is for you, but I'm sure that it exists for you.

We're all going to be hazed and razed in this time. My greatest prayer is for the people of conscience and the people of love to deeply search our hearts and souls in this time, and to make what we can of this search. I can promise that this is what I am engaged in.

This is what I am doing.

It is avant-garde to be so lonely
I forgot to send Lainey and Jaime their wedding
Gift. I haven't written that essay for Peter
What happened to me?
I applied for an apartment & it was offered
To me. I turned it down.
Last night I wept bitterly
Bent over my phone
Two toddlers, their heads bloodied
The mind of the world
The loneliness of our alphabet
My mind ceases to function
The loveliness of my alphabet
Somebody else carried the religion on their back
Somebody else died for the state
As for me it was "love" I wanted to die for
A womb cannot go against life
Even Vivian Silver, the famous peace activist
I feel I see supremacy in her living
Beside—even if working on behalf of—those her state
Subjugates. I am committing the error
Of judgment Michel warned me against. Putting
Myself above someone who has made a greater effort
Than I have to live her ethics. I think it is at least a little
Racist of me. All my friends seem to believe collective
 punishment
Is deserved. It is possible some of them believe they themselves
Personally deserve similar punishment. D studies
 punishment.

I wonder what she would say about our appetite for punishment.
I wonder what she would say about the appetite for punishment
Among prison abolitionists and intellectual critics of the State.

Not all psalms are created equal
Some are more beautiful than others
I have a new lover
He sent me a video of himself hoisting
A rock above his head on an overcast
Day, today in fact, on the edge of a lake
In rural Vermont
I felt the chill of the season for the first time
Today. Finally wrote F
He wrote me back
Immediately
On the news the grief on his face
Devouring him
I'm not on the news anymore, he said,
It's the system.
Crumbs and then ghosting

He writes of our sick culture
Like a jilted lover
He is in fact very gifted at love
Poetry.

"I am not doing enough" is what I hold
With greatest caution. The destitution
In me when I look at the horror
And exhaustion in my semi friend's face.
"I am not doing enough" is how I ate
Away at myself when Mom was alive, but poets
Have no right to metaphor in such a slaughter.

But I *did* destroy myself with that accusation.

But I'm not.
I ripped myself apart, I tore myself down—
Survivor's guilt. It's unproductive.

10/24/23

"A vapour went up from the earth, and watered the whole face of the ground."
—Genesis 2:6 (John Donne's version)

I awoke in liberty and in lightness and in small but purposeful independence and I must be my own subject from now on and magnify the fecundating humidities of my love.

What is this lightness? Momentary absence of fear. Absence of dread. If only momentary. Belief—what a word—in myself.

THE SCARLET WOMAN keeps appearing. Though today I also drew SORROW. I saw the sky pink over Stewart's and the Eastern light flooding what would become my small Hudson apartment with its view of the Speedway gas station. Except I can't rent that shitty little place.

October 22, 2023—Invisible College

I wanted to reach out with my voice. This nightmare seems to be convulsing the whole world and certainly has consumed me and many of the people that I love. I wanted to talk a bit about prayer, meditation, hypocrisy and the degradation of language in this moment. Ancestral agony has come alive in this world, the nightmares of our parents and our grandparents, for all, for all people who have been touched by genocide, and that's many people on the planet Earth. We are suddenly living in a horrific recapitulation of some of the worst things that our own families have experienced. This morning, I was corresponding with a friend, who is a great Palestinian-American poet. He told me this morning, an hour ago, that he's now lost fifty people in his family. Just a week ago, on his appearance on the news, a week ago, it was seventeen. All of this, these numbers are unimaginable. I don't know if I could even personally count fifty members of my family because my family was exterminated. This goes completely beyond my capacity to comprehend. Palestinians are being subjected to a level of suffering that sends me back to what my grandparents lived through.

It's very important, I'm noticing, for me to speak and share from an embodied place. It gets very easy to abstract and judge in this moment, specifically and precisely because it is so horrifying. It's very hard to stay inside the heart. This time has required of me a Talmudic level of self-study and attention. I'm relatively close to this war, this thing that's going on. Because I have Palestinian and Israeli friends that I love, and because my grandmother and mother loved Israel. But I am also far from it—because I am not Israeli, I have never been to that part of the world, I didn't and don't participate in Judaism in the ways most Jews I know do, and part of what I am trying to do is figure out how to be American and how to be my mother's daughter. And I am savagely trying to, desperately learning more, I'm reading more and studying more every day. A strange feature of a bloodbath is to also be studying its history and vectors via ten thousand think-pieces, interviews, books. You are in the horror and you are studying it.

Something that we study in Invisible College is the importance as an ethic to write from an embodied and from a heart-centered place. It's a matter of ethics, because it's easy to get imprecise, and to lose the essence of the thing when we start abstracting and intellectualizing. I'm not saying that we should take away our rigor or our precision, or that we should turn off our brains somehow. But we have to guard carefully, because the brain goes crazy with this stuff. It's being assaulted by absolute and total carnivorous brutality, and that breaks the mind down and the heart can't stand it. No human heart can stand to see what's happening right now.

Ancestral grief and ancestral nightmare, ancestral evil also, coming back to roost. This is something that's happening to each person, to every single person, no matter whether or not you are directly connected to the story that's unfolding. Or if you're just watching it, but still having a lot of visceral feelings about it.

And you know, that brings me to something that's difficult to talk about, which is the use value of this horror. This nightmarish conflagration, which feels like an orgy of death and cruelty is also a release point for grief and rage for the whole world. And this is why we're seeing people almost seize upon it with a lot of libido and appetite. Like there's some people who seem like to be almost devouring it with relish . . .

What we are studying is the feeling of truth as it moves through our bodies. What we are studying is heavenly mind. What we are studying, also, are structures, the structures of oppression, socially conditioned negativity, as they take root in and move through the body.

All this huge—societal—sociological evil—it comes from these small places and these narrow—carceral—terrible confinements of bad feeling—*in the body*.

When I teach sacred texts, when I teach poetry, I do so because I study these things for *information* about the structure of reality. This is not how it is done in the universities. This is not how I was taught. This is how I do it because I had to do it in order to keep my soul together given the insanity that was around me, and what the university offered could not do that.

This form of study is a way out of suffering. And we know

because we've studied these texts together, that these poems, some of them so old, some of the oldest poems that have been kept, from before there was even writing, we know these poems have real *information* for us—about the meaning of life, about the structure of the soul and body, about the dynamics and the functioning of the cosmos—which is extremely important. I don't know what could be more important.

And what is also preserved in these texts is that they act on the mind. They act on the whole psyche.

I decided to teach *Paradise Lost* this fall because in a flash of intuition late last summer I remembered Satan's rage against the sun. Milton's Satan hates nature, and he hates what is, he's against what is, he's against what is real. There's a way in which evil, for Milton, becomes this incredibly seductive and very real feeling of wanting to go against and go beyond nature—which is completely familiar for us personally and culturally because of the technological age we're living in. Satan's mistake was to forget that all of his power and glory comes from God. He felt like it came from himself.

Let me just read you a little bit of Satan shit-talking the sun:

> O thou that with surpassing Glory crownd,
> Look'st from thy sole Dominion like the God
> Of this new World; at whose sight all the Starrs
> Hide thir diminisht heads; to thee I call,

> But with no friendly voice, and add thy name
> O Sun, to tell thee how I hate thy beams
> That bring to my remembrance from what state
> I fell . . .

So Satan is talking to the sun and saying, I hate your beams because they remind me of the glory that I fell from.

> . . . how glorious once above thy Spheare;
> Till Pride and worse Ambition threw me down
> Warring in Heav'n against Heav'ns matchless King . . .

So it goes, on and on. One of the things that's interesting about Book IV of *Paradise Lost* is that we get to experience the introspection and the self-reflection of Satan.

Another thing that Milton keeps on doing in *Paradise Lost* is reminding us of freedom, that we are endowed with hearts and bodies and minds and we can reflect upon our experience with these. We have different forces fighting themselves out within us, we have different circumstances, we have different ancestries, we have different challenges. But Milton keeps on insisting on free will.

And I find this really helpful right now because it's not easy to keep one's balance, and we're all going to slip up and make mistakes. I made the mistake this week of thinking I knew enough to correct someone's perception on social media, or, even if I did know enough, thinking that doing such a thing was a worthy expenditure of energy.

I'm sure that I will make more mistakes. Because being in the midst of a metastasizing nightmarish situation that is drawing on very, very, very deep and ancient drives within the human system to loathing and murderous rage—one of the things about it is you long to get to a clean place.

You long to find a place where you're not soiled and befouled in the filth of this cruelty, of this unimaginable cruelty. And often where we go when we're trying to find a clean place is to a place of judgment, a place of intellect. So I have to keep on gently—rigorously, but gently—letting myself back into my own body. And really, really trying to stay with loving the people in my life.

If what I'm saying is abstract for you, let me try to be clearer—

When you notice yourself spiraling, focus on repairing what you can repair in your own relationships, in your own world and in your own day. I have to say that in my heart and in my body, I feel changed ever since acknowledging my father. It's almost pitiful: to acknowledge the proportions of one's own sorrow. Small as it is—it is my world. It's a reminder not to become grandiose in the face of overwhelming death and pain.

10/26/23

Café de Jaren, Amsterdam—

Forcing myself to write, as the war is engulfing me—
and everything. Strange to be in Europe again after
so long—and to recollect the thoughts I used to
entertain—that these are the friendly people who sent
their Jews to the ovens. Sickening violence continues,
devouring minds far from it, devouring my mind.
I awoke at three-thirty a.m. to take care of the Carol
Bove deadlines. Then was swallowed by yet another
group letter, and back-and-forth gorgeous conversation
with Harmony, but simultaneously growing more and
more agitated. The letter she signed, the letter before
that that I had signed, the feeling of immense pressure
that I should also sign this new letter, that it will be
loneliness or togetherness, that none of the letters I have
signed are as good as the letters I've written. That every
week there is a new letter and a new sense that chasms
are being opened up between me and my friends if I
don't sign every new letter.

Why don't I trust my own language and convictions
enough to make moralizing statements about what I
think should happen to a broader public? I can't even
convince the Jews on the listserv to somehow rally
against war. The hostage families don't want revenge . . .
Why do I devour myself? No one can stand this kind of
carnage. It will either drive you crazy or make you go
numb. Probably both. And you have to blame someone . . .

And you have to distance yourself from it . . . The only way to distance yourself, since it is flooding your phone and your body, is to try and position yourself above it morally . . .

Apartheid is a Dutch word.

Analogy, which the sun taught me about, is unfortunately an imprecise mechanism

And yet—it structures our mind

I'm looking at gray water. I'm looking at the black and white water transacting sunlight in its ripples

This quaint city full of bridges and bicycles, diamonds and jewels ripped like teeth from the jaws of the Earth

Waffles, hash, prostitution, slavery, colonialism, white supremacy

In this city Rembrandt painted Thomas's incredulity

Rembrandt, we are told, lived happily among the Jews

In my name, on some level, yet another atrocity is being committed

This has been the entire story of my adult life, politically

It messes with language, it messes with the integrity of one's feeling and being

And the further the mind is separated from the rest of Being from which it cannot in fact divorce

The more cynically you start to betray yourself in ten thousand little ways

Your sincerity has been undermined. You are not good enough to stand against evil.

You have been negotiating with it, selling yourself to it while complaining about it, minutely and yet with great

Grandiosity for too long, for far too long . . . to have any hope of standing "with" or standing "against."

You aren't standing at all. You are typing on your phone. You are overwhelmed by emotions you don't understand. You would put yourself above the horror you see . . .

I'm invited to sign yet another letter . . .

What do the governments of Qatar, China, Iran, the United States of America, Hamas, and Israel care if me and my friends ruin what remains of our love for one another? It would serve them well for our aggrieved little archipelagos of liberty to implode. I don't blame us for wanting to be better people than we are. But our fatuity and self-importance frightens me.

Doubled over in a dehydrated hunger that believes it still needs to prove itself . . . is there someplace I can grieve in secret . . . without putting myself above anybody . . . not even above my father . . . not even above the killers themselves . . .

October 27, 2023—Sex Negativity research group, Amsterdam School for Cultural Analysis, University of Amsterdam

I'm going to attempt to speak honestly with you about sex today. Because I notice that it's so difficult to speak honestly about it. It's almost impossible to speak honestly in public about anything .

There is a feeling we are protected by holding the right opinion. We're looking for language that can help us understand the dynamics that are real in our world and we're also trying to suffer less. Is that fair to say? There is this way of being honest and real and true about what life is actually like, but if you're only doing that in diatribes and manifestos, language very quickly becomes a tool for foreclosing upon possibility and expansion. We see that a lot right now. Language closes down very easily, it also forecloses thought and actually stops intimacy very easily.

Also degraded, or in the process of becoming degraded, is this artform of poetry, which anybody who has language can practice and in my opinion, should practice. It is a kind of hysterical moment with language that we're in, where now we can all see ourselves from every possible angle. And it is unclear how to use language now that we are all looking at each other and ourselves all the time.

For me, because I would not give up the kind of sex I wanted, even if it damaged my life, and in order to write about it, I had to forsake the language of theory. And I also had to basically abandon the popular discourse of my contemporaries and start studying sacred texts, ancient texts, in order to find help articulating what it was I was really after with intimacy.

My best friends were gay guys growing up, and when we were in our twenties they were beating each other up, calling the cops on each other, becoming addicted to meth, like, deeply, deeply enmeshed in the negativity of gay male "sexual practice," which sounds like the polite and academic way to talk about the way people actually fuck. I was also, at that time, really pushing my limits when it came to what I could physically and psychologically endure in relationships.

I involved myself in situations that led to me getting hit, assaulted, also very confused—but I did so completely willingly. I consented to all of it. For some reason my own negativity and that of my gay male friends made sense to me at that time. There was so much violence in their relationships, so much cruelty, so much loneliness, so much shame. I resonated very much with what they were doing—it felt like what I was doing—and I resonated with the kinds of literature that exist to describe such love.

I also think—there's a tremendous gap between our politics and the material reality of our sexual relations and our intimate relations. We want rights and respect, but in private we also long to be pushed beyond our limits, to be tested, sure, to be worshipped and adored—but also to be degraded and punished. Not just in a cute way. In a very heavy and serious way I would like one day to think through. The gap between our political/intellectual language about our sex and the space of our real desires and lives causes a tremendous amount of hysteria, and loneliness also.

Theoretical discourse that is meant to protect and dignify, I have found that it often attenuates the possibility of actual relating. It creates a kind of paralysis, when it comes to actually loving. It is too formal. All my life I had this incredibly melancholy longing for a femininity, like what I remember my grandmother exuding. Her femininity wasn't an idea, you just felt it. When you were in her presence, it made you want to make the world beautiful for her. And that was my masculinity, the man in me, the man who knows how to romance a woman, wants—to serve her.

You know, that's my gender. I don't know what that is. But that's my gender. I have this spirit in me—that is very affected by femininity. I could start weeping. I want to put my coat down on the ground and let her walk upon it.

I've noticed that creating weaponized discourses around sexuality has not worked, has not lessened the injustices people suffer. It has not made people happier, more intimate and free-flowing. It has not freed us from our addictions, it didn't stop my gay male friends from beating each other up or dying of their addictions, or coming very close to killing each other. For me, this weaponization of language and defense of identity is a reproduction of the war machine. Tanks and guns assembled around something incredibly wobbly and playful, emergent and alive.

And I've noticed, in the art world, whatever, we like sex, it is allowed. And thinking is allowed. But people's hearts are totally calcified. The heart is at present a taboo, it's become a taboo. It feels a little stupid, doesn't it? To talk about the heart? We don't practice speaking from it and we have no customs for speaking our hearts in public.

It's always connected to intoxication or excess or some kind of horror or accident—that a person speaks from her heart.

We're at a point in language as though we've become embarrassed by it. In so many ancient stories the world is created through language. And we also create our reality through what we speak. And so how much war-like self-animosity, loathing, loneliness, shittiness, insanity, are we also reproducing by our own embarrassment, and our own incapacity to use this gift of language with the kind of energy and commitment and love it deserves?

You could almost believe that the Devil had set things up to make human beings embarrassed by and disgusted with their own language, almost throwing up their hands that they can't even use it, that they cannot express their own hearts. I'm just going to say other people's slogans,

I'm just going to repeat other people's program. Because it sounds good or it feels right. It settles, it's settling in some kind of temporary way. Or I'm so terrified of saying the wrong thing, or thinking incorrectly, that I won't say anything.

The way that I feel my grandmother—and my mother—in my body, I miss them. I could start crying, I yearn for them. And I yearn for the feeling that they give me, which is a feeling of love and beauty, and that the world can be made beautiful enough to be worthy of them.

One can have less sex, for example, or less bad sex, but feel much more erotically flowing and fulfilled. Because one is suppressing oneself less. There's times in my life when I've preferred to cry than to come, for example. And times in my life when I've preferred to do mindless bodily things than have a really deep and satisfying conversation.

It's hard to cut into ideological language when it's just flowing through your phone and your body all the time.

That is what the cut-up does, it makes ideology more apparent. The cut-up, you'll all remember, was a creation of Brion Gysin that William Burroughs really popularized. It's something from the era of newsprint, when the language of the state had slightly more solidity—it was in newspapers and tax forms and magazines.

It's hard to do a cut-up with your phone, you know what I mean? The cut-up generated art that was meant to go beyond the ideological thinking embedded in public discourse in the sixties and seventies, and David Bowie used it to write songs and stuff like that. The cut-up was also a way of cutting into reality itself—cutting into language as it's flowing through the world in an unconscious way—and kind of opening up what is already there. There's anxiety around a word being fixed, there's all kinds of pain related and connected to language and all kinds of mental suffering. The ancients knew this and we know it as well. Something strange about language is that it is an unconscious flow, and yet it is also a space of great labor and precision and intensity—especially for writers and politicians. It is a vector of mind control but also, it expands consciousness.

I learned how to cut the line in my poems in a weird way, in Blogger comment fields. The line break is the most mystical thing in my experience of poetry, because poetry no longer has to rhyme and is much more open as a field than it used to be. Once I really found the line break in my body, it was like I'd entered the house of poetry. And before that happened, I had only been playing around.

Every poet breaks the line differently, because everyone has a different body. And because poetry is measured by speech and writing, it is made somehow at this strange intersection of writing and speech where you've said enough, or you've heard the sounds moving through you enough that you start to know where the sense of cutting the line is going to come.

The end of the line is like death and overcoming death, and enjambment is like a way of overcoming death, enjambment means the line is not end-stopped, so the phrase continues after the line break. Every line break is like overcoming your death, and it's like learning how to do it is intimately connected to your own breathing and your own body. I wish for every person this experience.

I said I would talk about sex, and now I am talking about death at the end of a line of poetry . . .

PORTUGAL

I made my way through Fátima alone. Stormy and overcast, El Greco skies, like the stern brows of its severe child saints

Cold rain blowing through bright shafts of sunlight, my heart kneeling . . .

I owe so much sanity to nail salons

Mass slaughter drained much of my will to live today, the sere winds of Fátima binding bloody cords of penitence around the waists of its children

I can drink espresso after espresso I still want to go to sleep

I am going to have to move my body

In some other way. You can move it across the world staying still

I trust myself, you, in this enterprise

I will try to write

I can try

I could love

Or my small musical gift

Or my physical gift

Which I humiliate in every poem

Let me therefore reconcile myself to such

And rectify my path such as I am able

Having entertained the heterodox monarchists of this strange social scene

All their thought still men's thought

BERLIN

Strange septic smells

Leaves in the corners

Evidences of a debauch

The same sun shines here

But they prefer it filtered

Thru black light

& a black dust of ground

bones smoked against the glass

I admit it made me sad to see her

Point her scanner at the fruit

I bought

Too many kinds of guns

In this country my problems are self-made

This is my privilege. Self-animosity too

Can be weaponized by the state. In the old

World it was the state murdering my family.

My pen just exploded

The old Paris

Spider coils of stairs

Up the bowels of the buildings

Haughty & ill-tempered

In light and timpani

Something like great poetry

Turning your midsection to steak

Cooking your blood

If anybody knows what's great it's these people

New Moon in Scorpio—en route to Prague

Pushing myself to write

Turbulence on the flight to Prague

The Paris reading ended in triumph

I nearly wept

There was a young man from Łódź

I mean his family was from there

I knew he was attracted me because he poked me twice and bought my book

We needed to show each other a little kindness

A young woman who had been ripping down hostage flyers

Brilliant and impassioned and very angry, she turned purple with emotion as we talked

And drove away the Jewish man with her fury

I had this fantasy we three could continue talking

I had this fantasy poetry could help us

What the hostage posters look like in Europe is not what they mean to the Israeli left

People outside Israel don't know there is an Israeli left

The only Israelis I know are of the left

Most of the hostages that were taken were of the left

I had this fantasy we could have stopped the war

Between the American left and the Israeli left

I tried writing letters to the leftist Jews on the listserv

About uniting the American and the Israeli left

But it turned out the leftist Jews on the listserv weren't that leftist

I would write these letters on my phone, doubled over, they were too long

And too soft, it was like pleading for mercy from my father

Terrorism has been used to justify global war my entire life

I have been sick with this my entire life

I am so tired of all the arguments in my phone

Somehow this tour is going fine

I feel like hell but I am putting everything into moving with a sense of grace and purpose

None of this was my idea

I ate a croissant from Paul with a hot black coffee

The Uber was an immaculate black Mercedes

Saint-Germain-des-Prés having become like a gray adhesive

I remember the old soaped Paris, the pockets within it where things stay "post-war"

Catholic and still with the old shames—losing to and collaborating with the Nazis

Many people in France live with shame and humiliation also because its meritocracy and management culture

Are so strict and racist, even scatological in their obsessive maintenance of their idea of dignity, and dignity's limits . . .

My pain was only distorted

By the curvature of the Earth

And soothed when I tried to organize it with my mind

Channeling it "correctly" into action or love

It was torture

I did not abandon my meditation

I did not consume drugs

Or give my body away

I stayed here in the wilderness with my phone

VANITY

Something at the gall-

Bladder point. No,

The spleen. "Sea

Of blood" inside and one

Hand above the knee—

Something slipping to the edge

Of me—always held me

Or so I felt, to one

Side, just shy of the line

Where beauty began.

"Beauty" was an inheritance

From our mothers, I want

To say. It was the form into

Which they sought to trans-

Substantiate their pain. As

We see it the form it takes

Echoes how they saw a form

That could bring them relief

From the volcanic emotion

Explosive love and un-

Reciprocatable hospitality

Their givingness brought

Into a world that never ceased

To overlook them, mispronounce

Their name, raise its voice

As though talking to an idiot child

Call their desires frivolous

Having killed their families

While dreading the bottomlessness

Of their gifts. I may have a serious

Contribution to make here. But

It is hard to see. Or beauty stays

Something you can't see (except in love).

Nobody taught me to hate

My own existence was a sin.

A spidery old woman gazes

Out from within a young body

To accuse the century.

Her terrible boyfriends and powerful

Girlfriends ricochet between father

And mother made by a body wending

Its way through the air, spinning

A home out of gossamer there.

It was a burning place. I remember

My cheeks hurting, distended

By a shoal of horns and boils,

Pancaked over in makeup I'd

Often sleep in, how I

Would never let a lover

Stroke my cheek or take

My face in their two hands

The history of love is hard

To write because it is made

Of the same intestinal pulses

That all bad things in this

World emanate from—the sparks

Of desire and mutual recognition

The giving to another the power

To render you meaningless

It's a consent the guts give if

Your parents don't teach you

Otherwise. Probably their

Guts flinched the same way.

Or you were born from happier

People than I was. I am older

Now and lovelier than I was then

Also tireder and the pictures

I see of me are still bad though I care less.

I do still care, but less.

My remaining vanity and what

Vanity has to do with self-regard

Anymore have been exhausted

By the horrors of the world.

Imagine caring what you look like

At a time like this. But I look around

And that's all I see. I might as well quote

Solomon himself. The people who can see

You for who you really are always could

Even before your plastic surgery.

They knew your true beauty.

In this time we have the right to adjust

Our bodies to make ourselves resemble

What we want to see. We also still moralize

And condemn—factors of interior

Mystery. I remember people making fun

Of Michael Jackson when he died

And I was crying. I remember thinking

If only he could have seen his own beauty

If only he had known how beautiful he already

Was before we stopped his heart. Whose heart

Could stand our cruelty? The human

Heart, I remember thinking.

The human heart, I thought.

The heart can only take so much.

When people selfie

They seldom look as good

Or as bad as they do in real life.

I've noticed I tend to be more attracted

To people who cannot fully see

Their own beauty and are thus protected

From interfering with it.

But nowadays you have to know

What you look like and to fail to exert

Some kind of control there, it's essentially

Crazy. OK another thing I remember

From when I was little:

Thinking you could basically be a writer

Without a body, or you could be really ugly

Or deformed and still you could do this.

As it turns out writing is insanely physical

And writers are as vain as everybody else

Only more complicated—our vanity runs deeper—

We are also morally and spiritually vain, politically

And socially. The cruel regime of Beauty

Made of several competing ideologies melted down

Into a single ore, rules all. Had nature made

Me complete I doubt I'd ever have begun to write.

I would have lived as music and trusted

The reality of my body. Years ago reading

Kafka's diaries I was consoled to find he too

Had hated his body, just like a woman

From the Twentieth Century . . .

October 28, 2023—rile* books, Brussels

Hi everybody, I'm sorry I was late—I fucked up the taxi situation. You all seem really relaxed.

(laughter)

I just want to say briefly this is an immensely overwhelming day, it's an Eclipse day. It's a terrible day and a terrible war. It touches many of us very viscerally and personally touches our families.

I want to also acknowledge this city has an important place in my and my family's history. Is it OK if I tell you my grandmother walked here from Berlin, she was liberated in Berlin by the Russians at the end of World War Two. And she walked here with two friends and was in a DP camp here. And when she was walking to the Polish embassy one day, she saw a man that she thought looked really Jewish. And so she asked him in German if he knew where the Polish embassy was, and he answered in Yiddish, I'm going there.

And that was my grandfather. Her husband had been exterminated. So the man she married was an ultra-Jewy-looking little man, my grandfather, and my uncle was born here in Brussels.

My grandmother used to tell me that the city was so clean that every weekend you would see the women of every building, they would be cleaning the street in front of the building, they would clean the stairs and also the streets. Is this true?

(laughter)

This is a story I grew up with but maybe it's all a lie. You're acting like people don't clean their own buildings and the streets outside their buildings in Brussels?

(laughter)

OK. Maybe things have changed. She used to talk about how filthy we were and what wild animals especially in comparison to Brussels where everything was clean, where the women would not only clean their own buildings but the streets outside their buildings . . .

I could go on and on like an old lady. But I won't . . .

I used to argue with my grandmother about Israel, throughout her life until she died. It was a source of sorrow between us. We didn't feel the same way about it. She really was of the belief that without the State of Israel, the Holocaust would happen again. She was of that generation. And she was of that experience. It's just a twist of fate that it happens that my family emigrated to the United States and not to Israel.

My grandparents and my uncle, and my mother was in my grandmother's belly—they entered the port of New York on my birthday, exactly thirty years to the day before I was born. And I only learned this last year after my mother died. I'm sorry to bore you with the family stories here, but it's strange because my birthday was just a few days ago and a friend of mine, who lives in Berlin and is very connected to documents—he's one of those people who always knows where all the documents are—he secured the disembarkation document from the boat my family took to go to America after the war. And I couldn't believe that it was on my birthday that they set foot in the United States. It made me accept for the first time in my life that I have a destiny with the United States of America, a place that I've never felt particularly comfortable.

But. I easily could have turned out Israeli. I just want to acknowledge that because I have never been to that country. And I think as a passionate, pro-Palestinian American leftist, whatever that even means anymore, I think I also felt a sense of superiority compared to Israelis, but maybe also some envy of their apparent self-esteem.

I feel like the room just went cold when I said that.

I've been confronting so many forms of grief, rage, powerlessness, disgust, self-disgust—racialized self-disgust—in these past weeks, and it's important for me to add, I suppose, a small précis about the misery of my little family. I've been wondering a lot about the future today. I've been wondering a lot about what it means to build a state out of so much suffering in response to so much trauma, and what kinds of evil that perpetuates.

And I wonder about what it means to build a state in response to the past. And what it means to build a state at all.

And whether it is possible really to live in one, fully to live . . .

NEW YORK

My sleep was so heavy, inside the meat of the world, dank and compressed and loaded with terrors.

Paid a debt two days ago. Many more to go.

Last night I saw the homeless man in the wheelchair outside my new building again as I was coming home.

It was cold, I found a quilt for him in my boxes, one I'd ordered when a lot of guests were always coming and I had that whole house upstate to myself—I brought it down.

He was bent over himself in the wind. I brought this for you, I said.

Just put it on me, he said, so I draped it over his shoulders and tried to cover his lap and legs.

Climbing the stairs to my new place I felt a tiny bit lighter.

In the morning the quilt was on the ground and the man was gone.

How is it so

Many bodies have sunk

Into the earth

So quietly

These billions of years

How did we never feel it?

Or did we? All that feeling

They keep telling you is nothing.

I felt it all my life.

They told me it was nothing.

It didn't even cause

A wind. Or did it?

Why didn't our teachers

Tell us this would happen?

Why doesn't this kind of killing afflict the weather here?

Why doesn't the Earth say something?

But it does. In your body.

"Not by might, nor by power, but by my spirit"
—Zechariah 4:6

I dreamed and slept a long

Time, its chalk coasts

Foamed in milky

Seas, seas that went turquoise

When you stopped looking at them . . .

Dreams of "retiring" from poetry

Is it the computerization of the planet

Or a loosening of my fidelity to suffering

I don't understand the intensity

I've hidden here but I know I despaired

Of finding a physical place to keep

My tears. Now what. Seas that go turquoise

When you stop looking at them. Just before 7

October we were dreading the computer

Stealing our life's work; our thoughts

Were of fighting the computer. But blood

Came back. Blood filled the computer.

I could only crush my soul as long as I could.

I made this art with what I could not crush but

I mistrust drama and its cultivation.

I am very suspicious of Story and Making

You Care. My suffering was stochastic

A speck in a field of data. I used to want

To be a ballerina but when my brother

Was locked up in Rockland I realized

Visiting him there—which I couldn't not

Do—would turn out to have been my arts

Education. I would have loved

To have been beautiful, to make

Shapes with my body or sing.

Instead I studied the Ten

Thousand Things and played occult

Tricks on myself that I was doing

As I pleased in absolute liberty

That there wasn't less beauty

In Port Authority than Carnegie

Hall, that my mind could become the jewel

To unite them both.

In resisting the drama of my own situation

I was trying to stop the war

I can't prove it in a court of law

You might have to feel it to believe me

To believe how wretched I was but also

How determined. Poetry isn't a profession

A person simply goes into. You have

To be fucked up to do this and especially

To stay. It does not attract the best

Or the brightest. We are some of the most

Sanctimonious low-attention-span narcissists

Around. But it gave me my life

Which I had a longing to see naked

And it held me up to living

In a very naked way

And showed me breathing

And gave me space

To find my way . . .

The ball of my left foot is bruised from a long walk home in heels on Saturday night. I was remembering the "health food" store I went into in Brussels. I was looking for almond milk. The man was on his prayer rug when I walked in. I waited for him to finish. I saw they had Quinton ampoules and that the store didn't have the air of a functioning store. Like not a lot of inventory, maybe more of a meeting place than a place of business. You know, one of those places like certain Italian cafés in Greenpoint the public just never enters, and they look at you weird if you walk in. We have things that can help with your skin the man said, pointing at his chin in reference to mine. No thank you I said, rejecting with a mild smile his assessment of my looks.

Immense vulnerability hangover with the outflow of my blood. Feeling fat, soft, exposed. The sun falls on my head like a priestly hand—the gentleness of its blessing is almost enraging—why won't it slap me, why won't it push me, why won't it force me to become better than I am.

Let's see if I can find the discipline to write this down—
or with my eyes open feel the things I felt this morning
under the covers before opening my eyes.

After the beauty of La Force at Webster Hall & a long
hang in the green room, I saw a little Lubavitcher boy
dancing that Hasidic ecstatic dance you sometimes see
them do—near Cooper Square. Usually the mitzvah
truck annoys me. It was cold and close to midnight. I had
my headphones on but I could see his smiling face trying
to get my attention—a redheaded boy with big prayer
tassels. "Are you Jewish?" Yes, I smiled, for once, and
wished him a happy Chanukah. He handed me a menorah and candles—and I burst into tears once I was safely
ten or so paces beyond him.

Judaism is like a cloth that was not cut to cover your
whole body.

It leaves you exposed and tests your love in vicious ways.

As small as a deadness can be—you prune it off—the flow is restored. Even the flow of a reconciled silence—a silence that comes to its end—

Nine thousand dollars are concealed in the shadow cast by the upper half of my body when I bend over. My home is an emanation concealed within these nine thousand dollars: I put my open palms together at the seam of the little fingers and cup my hands around the small place where my home hides in these nine thousand dollars, a secret I am trying not to harass and even harder not to betray, as I'm paying to live in someone else's house.

Lonely isn't the word for it, but I have the aggressed sensation of having found myself an instrument of glory and a footstool for the conquering hero. I deposited the fruits of my valiance at . . . maybe the wrong altar.

This is the second day I've achieved a real sexual fantasy. It's been almost a month since I felt whole enough to conjure anything like this.

Last night I walked until I found the moon. It was huge and comforting, hovering over a street that reminded me of Miami.

When the babies were put

Into cages at the border my mother

Was sleeping in my house. I had given

Up my house for her. This was the only

Way I could sleep during that time. But

Hardly stand. She is in the ground

Now. I saw her laid in.

And those children

Must be growing somewhere knowing

We all knew. We let that happen. Our

Wombs haunted by the thought of them

Our bodies were our dungeons and we knew

In our dungeons. It was the worst at night.

I started bleeding in self-reproach. "I too"

Know what it means to be ripped

From your mother at a young age

Maybe I grew up too fast to learn

How to wield my hastily acquired power.

Soul counts out its own deposition

Too many versions of this poem

Exist—where complicity gnaws

At the root of wisdom. Sentence

Lengthens if you fail to appear

Imagination stays in jail for a thousand more years

November 11, 2023—After 8 Books, Paris

I feel like I'm inside a tube, being squeezed slowly through it.

This is an unimaginably painful time. I don't even, can't even believe it.

I don't know how I'm even standing up right now, how we are here together.

Obviously, there's been thousands and millions of words, and I haven't been able to sleep, I don't know, for thirty-five days, I don't know anymore.

Last night I got my period and read Saint John of the Cross in the bathtub. I thought this ceremony would help me to at last achieve sleep but it did not.

So you have me at a moment of extreme liquidity— I'm in a liquid state. I don't say this to make a separation between myself and you. I have nothing to sell and no wisdom. This tour has no real purpose, there's no reason to do this, there's no point, there's no money.

It just somehow happened and I said yes. And so that's why I'm here for no reason. There's something to be said for doing things for no reason . . . I'm really grateful that you are here too.

This has been going on our whole lives. War.

When I first came to Paris it was the time of the protests against the War on Terror. And I was in New York on 9/11 but also my whole life, the crisis, the catastrophe of Palestine, the anguish of it was a huge argument between me and my grandmother, a visceral hell in my heart. But I don't want to make this about me. I'm here to read poetry to you. OK but that means I have to speak from where I am. So, I'm uncomfortable, and until I can situate myself in this discomfort it won't be possible to read poems.

One of the things that's been "interesting" lately is watching people try to know—try to act like they know—what the fuck is going on. And where all this is going to go.

But I feel like something so horrible has been happening for such a long time and it has seldom been accurately spoken of. It has always been very difficult to live with.

I honestly don't know. It isn't easy to seek a good life amidst so much moral decay. I've lost all my eloquence.

This is nothing new on some level. Except that we are watching it and carrying it in our bodies in a new way. Carrying the wrongness we always knew and felt, but heavier and worse and more.

What's new is the dilated compound eye of the witness of humanity. It's into this eye I put my prayer . . .

So, this fall I've been teaching Milton. And I think I have to talk a little bit about his eyes and revolution.

Milton went blind writing revolutionary tracts. He had had this youthful ambition to become a great poet and he ended up devoting himself entirely to the Revolution.

One of the things we can understand about *Paradise Lost* is it was a late work. He wrote it as an old man—in fact he dictated it, because he was blind. The lines would come to him at night. Milton destroyed his eyesight trying to bring about the end of monarchy, working for Oliver Cromwell. He was a Puritan, I should add, and being from Salem, Massachusetts I don't particularly love Puritans . . . It's not a legacy that I want to tune into necessarily.

But the kind of Puritan Milton was feels very different from the kind of Puritans that came over on the *Mayflower*. Milton does not hate sex, nor does his imagination shrink from science, and he definitely does not seem to loathe the feminine, or women specifically, though things do get complicated between the Serpent and Eve in the Garden . . . Milton wrote his greatest work as a man who had lived to see the total collapse of everything that he had fought for, politically and socially and spiritually.

Paradise Lost contains the up-to-date science of the day. Milton sees the cosmos through a very unusual optics of space–time. He even visited Galileo. You might know that Giordano Bruno was put to death for saying that all the stars in the sky could very well be suns, around which planets like our own were orbiting. And Milton says multiple times in *Paradise Lost* that Earth is a pendant suspended from heaven—but that there could very well be other worlds—a.k.a. alien life on other planets—within the scope of God's creation.

He refers to God scattering, sowing the stars in the sky like seeds. And I'm particularly interested in this, because in a lot of the ancient texts I study, farmers are unloved by God. God loves shepherds, but the farmers are cursed in many old stories—Cain and Abel maybe most famously. God loves shepherds. Farmers are somewhat cursed. And yet Milton has God scattering stars in the firmament, like a farmer.

It's really interesting to me that Milton's able to conceptualize life on other planets—other worlds—back in the seventeenth century. Just last summer there were congressional hearings in the USA about alien spacecraft, and the culture basically shrugged. Our minds and imaginations seem somehow stretched out and deadened.

Working on this epic has been a way to kind of get underneath and behind some of our received ideas about masterpieces, revolution, Science vs. God, the limits Christianity may put on the imagination—in so many ways Milton himself created tropes we think of as much more ancient. *Paradise Lost* has reminded me how fundamentally heroic a compassionately imaginative act can really be.

It has also reminded me that it takes great imagination to take on the problem of evil on this Earth—and the mysteries of destiny and free will—even if you're going to tell fairy tales about all this stuff, to really take it on and wrestle with it is an invigorating task.

I'm not saying the book is perfect, or unmarked by Milton's very particular personality—but it is just undeniably a miracle of the imagination, and in so many ways we are still living in ideas the poem put into the culture we've inherited. Ideas that don't actually come from the Bible, or the English crown, or the scholars in the academies—but that come from the immense imagination of the poem itself.

It's been steadying for me, even though I have not been able to sleep, and even though I've succumbed to a lot of self-torment in the face of what we're all seeing.

We think of ourselves as being stuck in this horrifically ancient hell that is becoming totally technological, but I feel like Milton's mind was more flexible than ours are, even though we've seen so many more things than he did.

And in a way, the hell realms of the human mind have always been very bloody, and very robotic also.

Well, there's no good way to do this really. I have to pray in order to function these days and I find I'm always looking for a witness inside me that is somehow above me that can help me see everything—all the horrible things I have to see—and not be damaged by them, or let them turn me evil or crazy. I believe that this witness exists, I do believe that witness exists. OK. Glad I got these things out in the open.

The poetry reading is starting, you can relax now . . .

Something I had always wanted: to see my life itself, like a white flame, a nothingness. To really stare it in the face . . .

*

This war must be driving people insane. All of us watching.

It takes all I have not to be driven insane by it, and I am—here comes a word I've come to loathe because of the way the powerful use it, because of the way the powerful use it to describe people they don't give a shit about—I am *resilient*.

*

"Resilience" is a word the powerful use to describe the peoples and populations they have yet to destroy, yet refuse to help. The vampire praises your resilience— then sinks his teeth into you.

*

My mother's death might have liberated me. But I fell back again and again into politics and the mind of war. I became enraged at other Jews, while constantly being forced to confront, also, my own bigotry against them.

I took refuge in music and went back in time, traveling deeper and deeper into Europe.

What have I been hiding in my body as I've moved through the old world, the places where my family was destroyed, the places where my family began . . .

Among other things, my sword. The one I wield against myself. A secret shame of mine . . . an out-of-date ritual . . .

※

I have just received a photograph showing what I looked like the last time I lived in New York. Just before I gave Mom my apartment.

I was so divided against myself then. It hurts me to see. Couldn't anybody see?

I resemble in this image the "ratlike" creature I wrote two poems about, whose extinction in Australia had been announced the same week as the massacre at PULSE.

I remember thinking—it was 2016—I am such a rat.

"A ratlike rodent" was how Amy Goodman put it. I thought of Roberto Bolano, Kafka's Josephine, Mickey Mouse, and Art Spiegelman.

At what point did I consent to sharing the universal mind of vermin and outcasts?

I found it very very difficult to live with myself while my mother was alive.

I couldn't give up the habit of blaming myself for her condition—but I reproached others for it too.

I could never achieve enough peace with myself to "accept" myself—but neither could I raise my rage to the heights of purity.

It killed me slowly. To be divided against oneself is a sickness.

That's a misuse of the sword.

The sword and how to use it: Let me indulge for the last time in a tiny orgy of self-cruelty.

My face was like a knife cutting into the woman I longed to be.

There was something insect-like and cutting that also partook of the rodential in who I appeared to be—teeth gnawing through the dark—and a misshapen compound eye and sectioned body—a thriftstore fur, my lover's sweater, a red manicure, and a woowoo ring of selenite—my aura was full of holes. My left eye did not match my right. My sentences hardly understood themselves. The planes in which my hair fell across my brow did not agree with the right eye and the left. My features only made sense one at a time. All you have to do is look at this picture and you can see a person vivisected, trying to hide from one part of her body the conflagration in the other.

At a loss for harmony—searching for some way to visually reconcile an inner war. I also look like a woman trying to prevent herself from turning into a four-legged creature or a wizened bird of prey. As though she could stop it from happening. I look like a monster trying to fit into society. Like someone changing so rapidly she has no idea how to make it all work as a "look." A woman in the process of becoming a bird. Not a voluptuous bird. A raptor.

Body as lean-to, body as makeshift shelter.

Homeless people always noticed me in those days. Especially the women. I resembled them. They liked my style.

PERSONAL ESSAY

The navel is an eye

Every hole in the body is

Even without love

Even after all this time

My body continues to generate real, healthy, human emotion

So much is manufactured to subvert it

Even this morning

Tears on my face

I have not gone numb

This is victory

Tho it also means I remain

Vulnerable to manipulation

I have a friend who wrote a novel

About "invulnerability to coercion"

The protagonist has to drop

Out of society

In order to maintain the autonomy

Of his mind and way of living

Some of us spent the last ten, twenty

Years romanticizing such acts

Of rebellion. My way of dropping

Out was to stay moving, constantly, THROUGH.

How is it "we all" are so wounded by the facts

Of our culture and how is it "we all"

Still feel so alone "with" it? Like a screaming child

Left alone in its soiled diaper. Orphaned by this culture.

And to it. The world has required, at different periods,

Innocence

For its redemption. Or if you prefer

A less loaded word:

For its refreshment.

Or was it "innocence" that triggered

You? My rage and cynicism were socially produced

And I used them only against myself. This I *could*

Prove in a court of law. Some things that should not

Be complicated have become so.

You can't even butter a piece of toast

Or drink a glass of tea innocently

Iniquities and hypocrisies live in every cell

Of your appetite, the proportions you set

For your little life. When the soul tries to distance

Itself from sickness like I noticed in the faces

Of the orderlies when my brother

Was in the mental hospital and also in the faces

Of the guards when my mother was on Rikers

It hardens and dulls. It's something medical.

Not to catch what the people you're guarding

Have wrong with them. I want to distance myself

From the killers. They do disgusting things

I would not do. They use ideology to justify it

And so on. Their souls have left their bodies

And so on. But I want to end the war. My teacher

Told me to beware of judgment

The fact is it was judgment I had been feasting on

To put myself above the people I believed—believe—
are wrong

Beware of judgment, my teacher told me, and he was
right.

Now his country is engulfed

In the chaos he told me for years would come.

It is somewhat calming to intellectualize horrors like this

And try to sort out with your brains how they could
have happened

We should study something other than the brain and what we agree

To call discrete facts. I would rather be one

On whom no miracle would be wasted. I would become

A place where war would be impossible

But if I hated myself, could not control my appetites

Could not help but hurt the people

I loved, If I displayed my talents narcissistically,

Indulged in vapidity and vainglory

How could I expect better of my culture? Something very

Young in adults is being drawn out by the witness

Of suffering and I admit

It disturbs me. Something eternally young

But not in a good way. Child in them

Ravaged and very hungry and wanting

You suffering with them. The watcher

Becomes consumed with her own pain.

But am I succumbing to judgment, writing these lines?

Her own pain overwhelms the bleeding

Child in her eye. She only hears the child

In her: the rich hypocritical one that paid for the bombs.

I am in pain, says the voice all around me,

I am in pain, says everything I see

Everything I see says, Don't leave me alone

DISINHIBITOR

There's a sadness I'm avoiding

It's why I live like this

The truth is I know I can't hide

From it. I know I can't

But I *can* hide from you

Or I somehow still think I can

& what that really means is hide *it*

From you. It's not that I don't trust

You. I'm just scared to lose

It. I'm not avoiding

My sadness I'm trying

To protect it. What I lost

I already lost a really

Long time ago. Whatever

I tried to do apart

From what I lost had more

To do with covering it

With probably some kind

Of monument than "moving on"

But I'm the only one who needs

To know that it's a monument

Or what it's for. Ant hills

Mountains out of molehills.

Growing a roughness into

A jewel: Aphrodite's secret.

I am ignorant of my people's

History but I have seen the scrolls

In their crowns and gowns.

The times I won I wasn't able

To celebrate. So I learned equanimity

But equanimity's as tricky

As any other state. These may

Not be words of wisdom

But they've got no other

Place to live

I find this country cold

Walking room to room clutching

At my heart thru the cage

The only thing warming this country

Is the people who come here from other places

& the people brought here

Against their will. That's how it feels

Today. Day of atonement.

My father became identical to his oppressor

Is one way I've heard it put. But

That kind of concentration on one's own

Interior suffocation makes the eyes

Pop out in a particular way

I have learned to recognize

They will try and make you believe

Soul death is a slow and gradual process

That's a lie. You have to work

To kill it. Actually it can't be killed

But it can be driven from the body

To wander the world like a wind

Still. It takes tremendous effort

To make it leave home. Today

It is very very windy.

They used to have wooden

Tables here. This one is

Plastic. It doesn't sit

Right, what you're

Offering me. What you

Want in exchange for what

You're pretending to give me.

My feet and root

Find something in the ground

To orient my movements to.

I'm getting really tired

Of the argument you're having

With each other. The change

You are talking about bringing

About is already here. You,

The slow ones, the rich

Who abjure such work will capitalize

Upon what we've been doing down

Here without understanding it.

Without changing yourselves.

Your kind have always existed.

You have never changed.

ECLIPSE

lightness of being

it may be

none of this death & suffering

means what "we" think it

means

doesn't matter whether "we know

what it means" or not

it should stop. why can't we stop it

those who love humor more

than the mortgaged people

timing out their breaths

in emergency houses

for this is emergency too

untouched, unknown,

in a kind of pain that can't be spoken

this orgy of suffering draws us out

of our private little hells

it draws all our pain out and magnetizes it

and to master the horror of it

we spew opinions, judgment and rage

i too do it

everyone is doing it

I believed I was understanding
what I was seeing.

I dreamed I was renting an apartment in Eileen's
building. Somehow it was the attic—the top floor.
In "three days" I managed to make a mess of it. I felt
hot shame when Eileen walked in—I'm about to clean
this up, I said. In the air the genocide was palpable.
I was conscious of myself sleeping while children were
marched to their deaths, dying of thirst. My friends
sent me poems of Darwish, asking if this was the last
night on Earth. I was conscious of my body sleeping in
a rented bed, far from the atrocity. The atrocity went
on in my body, around which no human being encircled
their arms. My right hand found my left hand. I was after
all in the town where I first learned to be alone. I love
you, I said. I love you too, I said.

The feeling of moral failure—of unbeauty—as I know it—always goes back to my mother.

My ability to walk past homeless people, to rely upon my headphones piping Bach into my brains not to break my stride when I feel the deranged aura of a street person moving importuningly toward me . . .

I came of age knowing that like all people—at least like those that surrounded me—I longed for beauty, knowing that in my soul I was hypocritical and small.

I was capable of spasms of insight and occasionally, real goodness. But mostly I punished myself, and tried—only halfheartedly—to hide it.

I think I tried harder to show it.

Take me . . . understanding

From grief. That was just the redness

Of my whole people falling thru me

Coins of black blood at the bottom of the bowl

Dreaming myself into the snow of Syracuse

Learning to write prose

I may have a name but I don't know anything

About America yet

What kind of a woman's natural resonance

Is the heavily shamed testimony of her womb?

Terry taught me that too is land

I turn my back on my land

And head toward the city

In search of work . . .

Its lights, smell of detergent

Gray water & chicken bones

Remembering how to fold my body

Into a linoleum corner

Somebody's black hairs blow

Like bugs across the floor

"And the bondage of the body is severe."
—*The Paraphrase of Shem*

Penitentiary approaches to change

Tending toward isolation as strategy & habit

I haven't been able to sleep

It rained today amid slots of sun

Got my nails done having resolved

To become a friend to myself

I've noticed I hide from things

& people even when I commit

Immense energy to move toward them

It's a mechanism

I recognize again & again

As "self-preservation" but that's too simple

Because I hide also from my own gaze

& also from the page. This is neurosis

I have no wish to dignify.

I will not simply disregard, with a wave of my hand, what these atrocities do to me—what they do to me in the most private and unspeakable ways—what they do to me and what they may also do to you.

The work of intellectuals to moralize, to denounce, to articulate clear positions and to make specific political demands—I respect this work. I mean—I suppose I respect it.

But they hide too much of themselves in their moralizing and that's what frightens me . . .

We should show ourselves . . .

I am doing something perhaps sickening and internal.

Something that I think—I hope—might also mark some meaningful contribution to a moving-away from necro-imperialist posthumanism.

I wrote these notes when swamped by horror and shame; they respond an ethic of non-self-abandonment.

As "vulnerable" as I have so often been accused of being—

It takes enormous strength not to run away from oneself—

No one has the right to say what or who I am but me

No one but me has the right to abuse me

Preliminary materials toward a theory of sovereignty . . .

I am refusing myself the synecdoches and conclusions I see many friends drawing.

It is not that I don't see the evil of the settler-colonial project. It's that I have no reason to trust "us."

Not yet, anyway.

Well it's fitting that I'm bleeding as I write you.

Because otherwise I'd forget—the way I always want to—the way I do every month—that it's my soft, underresearched tissues that are probably the crux of the matter.

Or at the very least—near its heart.

You forget on purpose, over and over.

It puts you in a different world.

It should be the least alienating thing in the world—but "we" only talk about it when "we're together" and "feel safe to."

The world of "the natural"—the world of all other immensities waved away with a stroke of the pen or a reductionist slogan—an endangered world—a world I hide and protect with the bulk of my body and with the gifts I work to give to this world.

Settled history is an edifice constructed and policed by those with a stake in how it tells power. Someone should write a history of menstruation and how it has been treated and understood. Imagine Foucault having done such a thing. Imagine a gay male philosopher's history of menstruation taking its place beside his histories of sexuality, madness, and punishment.

Imagine the cycles of the egg being studied *as consciousness*.

I won't, in my dread of power, worship victimization—it's a terrible power that rolls thru my body as heat and red. It is transpersonal, transhistorical, parapsychological, and paranormal. It is fertile, virile, febrile, and strange. It is a sign of health—voluptuous and sometimes agonizing to experience.

If that is not power what is.

In speaking of it I am not requesting that attention or respect be paid it.

I would not ask you for anything, whom I do not know.

Maybe my desire is to break a taboo within myself and dare you not to have a problem with it.

If it weren't a taboo, more people would talk about it.

Menstruation is not an idea. It is not a concept.

It is a fact, a phenomenon, a rhythm, an experience of violence, shame, and pain. It is an experience of time. It is the soul of time.

The stiffness & cruelty of war & its language—by they who wage & justify it & by we who oppose it—

My blood grieves it

THE FRONTIER

I felt a pressure not

To write. How

Can I explain it.

It was as though

Embarrassment

Had been connived

Into language—

Which could not any

More receive

Reality neutrally and, well,

Express it. For me. I felt

Yes, I am writing but

It wasn't accurate.

There was something in the world

That hadn't been named

Or studied—a kind of suctioning

Action mostly at the border

Of my perception and just beyond

That did not need to communicate

Directly to me for its force

To be felt by me. I had trained

Myself to resist whatever

It was, for years. Even this

I don't know how to explain.

My troops were at the border. But

After a while things got confusing

And I started feeling tired all the time

Wanting to lie down in the road

Or just stay in bed which

Was also a form of resistance

Or so I was told and even

When I was feeling vigorous

And cultivating desires—because

If you don't want anything it's hard

To move your body—I felt something in me

Always wanting to speak or sing

Tell my lover something

I wouldn't end up knowing

How to tell them, that when

I wrote it down it also just did not

Feel accurate, and this went on for years

Until a cultural phenomenon caught up

With me and now shame and cruelty clung

To words and they no longer seemed godly

And my experience of the world stayed inside

The world, never reaching the threshold

Of its transformation, never reaching your ear

However you might name the edge where all I feel

Drops off into infinity, canyons, a hole

To put it mildly—this frontier—

The place from which I write you

A light year in the future

From where I perceive the grid

Of our developments and ideas

Eaten away at and gouged by hands

Of wisdom and also of rage. From

Where I perch like a bird.

From where our yearning used

To meet the beautiful languages of our century

And from there, into our bodies

Or did the feeling hit our bodies first

And trust and love make understanding?

Is there such a thing as loveless telepathy?

I don't think I'd want it.

The way my man friends spoke of the future

It sounded like a dead neutrality in which their ideas

Would enjoy free play.

The child's head presses down

At the door of the world. The cow's horn

Prods infinity. In infinity the cow eats patiently

Beyond the sounds that shape the mouth

And borrow the air for our voices

I lost faith in my strength to say it

And lost trust in your desire to hear it

I stopped hoping my father would call me

Eventually I had to accept that I also

Could not call him. Silence

Is golden. Silence is dignified.

A picture is worth a thousand words.

There was a vogue for silence in writing

Among adults when I was younger. It was taken

To be the correct consequence of slaughter

And those art works and forms that figured

Out how to contain this silence were considered

The great ones. "How can a secret

Be known as a secret," asked a now

Forgotten philosopher. It is no

Exact science how a world takes form.

We know the old books speak

Of the word

Splitting the darkness. Gods seem

To recede for lack of love—they begin

To resemble ghosts; forgotten history

And also the distortion of something

Talked-about if you never get

To hear anything better than the talk.

So. The female form representing

Universal wisdom is fashioned

And refashioned again. "We never

Learn" is true in a way. But truer

Still the monument to a kind of time

That does not age. If you feel

It then you know

November 4, 2023—Hopscotch Reading Room, Berlin, with Ghayath Almadhoun and Bill Martin

When I first heard Ghayath read I thought, I have to quit poetry.

Truly. I wrote to Bill in the middle of the night and said, I think I've heard a real poet for the first time in my life, and I immediately became paranoid about the feeling, because I'm a Scorpio. I thought, I haven't heard real poetry all these years until now, and I thought, I should eviscerate myself, I should suicide my entire art.

Then I became racially paranoid.

(laughter)

I immediately thought, maybe there's a secret djinn in the poetry of this great Palestinian poet that causes Jewish poets to want to destroy their art. I mean it seemed completely logical at the time!

(laughter)

OK, I'm very nervous.

(laughter—reading begins)

OK. There are tears on my face, as some of you can see, and I don't drink but I've honored this special occasion by getting a little drunk. This is indeed a very special occasion. And I want to thank you—all of you—for this ceremony which I personally required for the persistence of my soul at this time.

I could not have lived without this. I'm very, very grateful. I'm about to significantly diminish the register, poetically, by reading my own poems. But before I do I need to say, I have to speak from my womb because it feels taboo at this time to do so.

If you don't mind.

I have a friend, Jaguar Womban, who teaches that in this world there's only one womb. There's just one. And those of us who "have" one, we are of the one, the only one.

I feel my mother and my grandmother very much lately in my body. I only trust the language that somehow comes through them—through me.

And of course they—my grandmother and my mother—hate war.

Every mother hates war. My grandmother was a slave in this city. And after the liberation, she and her only friend who was also Jewish, they knew because they had come out to each other as Jews, they barricaded themselves in their rooms because the Russians who liberated the city were also raping everybody, as you all probably know. And after the war, they walked from here, from Berlin, to Brussels.

Last week on the day of the Eclipse, I was in Brussels, the city where my mother's family began. It's very strange for me to be here. Now. It's a complete coincidence, really, it's the way things happen, it's all just a happenstance.

My book was out three years ago, my tour was canceled by the pandemic. And a few weeks ago the launch of Ghayath's new anthology was canceled—by cowardice— so here we are, thanks to Bill and Siddhartha and Erin.

I wish somehow that this could be the last genocide we witness on this planet. I don't even know what the right prayer is, at this point. Do you know what I'm saying? And I'm saying things that I wouldn't be able to say if I weren't delirious with jetlag and exhaustion. And if I hadn't drunk two glasses of white wine out of a paper cup, and had you not just heard these astonishing poems of Ghayath's. And you're all being very generous with me. And I thank you.

My mother died on November 17 of last year. She committed suicide. She was schizophrenic.

One of the reasons—one of the many reasons—I adore Ghayath's poetry is because I myself am an adrenaline junkie. The book he's reading from is called *Adrenalin*.

Some of us are adrenaline junkies: I'm looking for other faces in the room that light up. Yes, I see you. I see you.

(laughter)

These things make us a little fucked up. It feels taboo, even to do what we're doing here together tonight, actually kind of Kumbaya, like it's not really being done right now, if you've noticed.

The memory of adrenaline comes from terrible things— and the appetite for it also.

And therefore I want to say a few words on behalf of poetry. And on behalf of not getting killed, even though I understand why Ghayath expressed some feelings of guilt over having stayed in Europe writing poetry.

This feeling, of course, one experiences it as cowardice, but poetry is a very strange and persistent thing. It's something that was created for moments like this. And it does require your survival in order to practice it. Though survival and poetry can at times gnaw at the body like cowardice.

Poetry endures longer than anything, actually, if you think about it, longer than states, and cultures, and religions and peoples and all of it. Poetry endures and outlives evil and stupidity. Isn't that strange?

And not only does it endure, but in these times, it gives life. I find it very strange that it's poetry that has given me life. I just don't understand how that has happened. I don't even like it that much—

But part of its mystery as an artform is that it requires

your participation. I wish to say a few more words on behalf of poetry.

Anyone with language can practice this art. It is the most naked of all the arts. It requires no equipment. It requires no friends. In some ways, it thrives on the lack of friends. But it also loves friendship—it loves love. And yet it can do without everything.

You know, you don't even really need to know how to write or read to be a poet, although reading and writing enrich it.

It is a life-giving practice. It is something with energy in it, it is something with life in it that endures. It's not only for the professionals. It's a matter of being human.

And therefore it was not cowardice on Ghayath's part to want to live and write poetry.

Your poetry is required here, your presence here is required. It's a very awkward thing to be at this post, at the post of poetry, to be like, OK, reporting for duty—here I am. This is incredibly agonizing, and also somewhat embarrassing work. That's how you know you're really doing it.

This world, they say, was created through language, and I do feel that we're living in a time where we are being made to feel very embarrassed by this faculty.

We are being shamed out of language.

We feel very embarrassed by this faculty of speech, constantly having this feeling that we don't know how to use it, that we're doing it wrong, we don't know how to trust ourselves within it. We don't trust ourselves to constitute reality reliably within it. This is something that is happening that is part of the war. It's part of the war. And it is being done to everyone. We are not being bombed and slaughtered but our sense of constituting reality in our speech and writing is being assaulted.

Just as we can be defiled by circumstance, by horror, we also can defile ourselves by what we speak. We can use evil language that was designed to deaden our minds and kill our hearts. I see it everywhere.

And I notice that in this time of outrageous slaughter, outrageous, obscene slaughter, I notice that people are doing things in language that I see as a representation of their attempt to find a cleaner place to be. A more sanctimonious, a more morally above, a more—whatever—because the pain is unbearable.

Actually, what we are seeing can't be borne.

And even feeling the "right" way about it can't make it bearable. Shouldn't.

And it is happening to all of us, which potentially could be revolutionary, but I don't mean that in the way of chanting slogans, I mean that in the way of the heart.

This time should not be tolerable.

There should be no profit and no glory from this time. It is a time of great humiliation. And I have to say, I never thought, I never thought that when I would come into adulthood, it would be inside an age of the slaughter of children.

Will you forgive me for saying these things?

I'm going to continue, I have to continue. God forgive me. I am with you.

I never thought that my adulthood would emerge into an age of the slaughter of children, not only in Palestine by Israeli bombs, but also children killing children in my country, in the United States. This has been an era of the slaughter of children. And I'm saying this with intent. The child is a total person. It's a total human being, it's a total being. Those of you who are parents know this completely, you know this completely. But everyone who's ever been born knows it too. If you kind of sink down deep into the somatic memory of who you were, as a small person, you're a total consciousness.

What's very interesting about the gates of the human incarnation, is that we come in once and we go out once.

We come in through the door of the womb.
So far, everybody here came in that way, I think, including the aliens and the Ascended Masters. You came through

a womb. The one womb, the one. And for me, when I buried my mother last year, I have to tell you it was the most important thing I've ever done in my life. I've never done anything more important in my life than burying my mother with dignity. Jews also wash the body. I gave my mother an Orthodox burial. And in many ways, I was kind of like her father or her husband, I don't know what the incarnational mishmash is, whatever. Because she was very sick the last twenty years of her life.

Of course, it's an outrage when any human being is killed. It's commanded by God, you're not supposed to do this. It's a big mistake to kill someone, one person, one person. But especially the elderly, and the children, they're completely dependent on others. And that is part of the way this whole thing is set up. Giving to a human being the love and the dignity of a full human being when it is not within its power to do that for itself. In other words, the care of babies and children, the care of the elderly and the dying, this is sacred. The dignity and importance of it are unfathomable. This is completely sacred. You cannot escape the importance of this work.

We are forgetting how to do this work in my country. We are giving up caring for ourselves and for each other. We are watching the slaughter we pay for, and we are giving ourselves away in the process . . .

I went out of my body
Into the war

But you know—

I could be wrong.

I could be wrong about all of it.

How can I describe what that time was like?

November 26, 2023—Invisible College

I am home, which is something that I have not been able to say for a long time.

I rented a little apartment in Little Italy, kind of Nolita. I had a series of events in—let's see, can we go through the trajectory: Amsterdam, Brussels, Lisbon, Berlin, Paris, Prague—and then an event in New York City at the Met on my mother's death day.

The whole tour didn't have really any material purpose. And it cost a lot. It cost everything I had, financially and spiritually, to do it—but I knew it would.

Do what costs the most, wrote Simone Weil.

There was an alignment to the whole thing. It was set up before we knew there would be war happening. But then again, there was already war.

It was an extremely painful journey, through the darkness of the Holocaust, seeing the manifestation of this energy—this genocidal mind erupting again. Not that it has been gone—it's been smoldering and festering in the world in the same wounded bodies, and the same wounded minds and lineages for as far back as we can think of.

But it has blown up in a way and on a level, on a scale that we've not seen in our lifetimes. It was extraordinarily painful to be alone traveling through those places, but it was also something I can't imagine having let anyone do with me.

But the tour was also incredibly, incredibly beautiful on a personal level, because it put me in contact with people who were in the same pain that I was—it forced me out of myself. The dirtiest trick of this culture is that you are alone with your sense of injustice, that your sorrow should isolate you.

I would not have believed the censorship that is going on in state-funded institutions, in small institutions and nonprofits. I would not have fully believed it if I hadn't put my body *into* these other places, where they have other histories and norms and governmental styles. In particular, Germany.

All of this censorship, I believe, is calculated to foment a frame of mind of perpetual war.

And I actually think it's really, really important for artists—artists of the wrong race, or of the right race, or of whatever—for artists of this moment to be working and talking together and exchanging ideas. And if that means that certain execrable ideas and certain hateful forms of expression come through, I would prefer freedom of speech to censorship.

I believe that the censorship we are seeing—and in many ways also participating in—plays directly into the creation and perpetuation of the mind of war. A mind of hatred. This creeping experience of censorship from outside *and* inside also opens the consciousness and the mind to these insidious forms of loathing and distrust that creep in as we are absorbing so much horror.

I'm living outside and against a lot of the trends and the currents that exist in this culture already.

I can't submit a resignation letter to *The New York Times* or *Artforum* or my university, because I've already resigned. As you know I sued a major university following an experience of sexual harassment that came two years before MeToo, and that's how I became a full-time astrologer.

I've already withdrawn my labor from a lot of the exact places people are quitting from—and getting fired from—now.

I got comfortable owning next to nothing—it was how I protected myself from my mother. The things I gave her—my home—I mean, that was agony. It ripped me apart, and it took getting used to. But over time I gradually learned the benefits of liberty . . .

My trajectory—vis-à-vis the ways that these institutions function—has already been, for a long time, a trajectory of agile wandering to the best of my ability, and I did this for my own physical health, because being inside of those structures was also making me sick.

And I'm here talking to you right now, also, because I'm someone who has had overpowering mystical experiences. And I don't say that to make myself special, or to put myself above anybody else. These experiences are here to be had, by all of us, by anyone who wants them. We don't yet have social structures or conventions for how to talk about and share and even learn from the mystical. It's not something up in the sky, it's something very physical and real that also changes one's perspective on the structures and norms that order our culture.

Lots and lots of people experience things like the ones I've had to very patiently train myself to talk about, and very gently reorganize my life around. I do think that *wanting* such experiences—wanting miracles—is a big part of experiencing them.

Having experienced such things, it behooves the experiencer to cultivate and create an active relationship with these new regions of consciousness—or else they'll just close back up.

You have to do that yourself because "society," so called, is not set up to keep you in tune with the most magnificent and magnanimous experiences of life. "Society" is set up to estrange you from yourself and to separate you from goodness. The goodness inside you and the goodness around you.

I'm here talking with you right now, in connection to and in continuum with these dynamics. I had these late-night conversations with Ghayath Almadhoun in Berlin about politics and geopolitics, terrorism and dictatorship, that were some of the best, most honest, least racist conversations I've had about these things with anyone, ever and it's partly because he's one of the least racist people I've ever met. And he also is constantly joking he is seventeen percent Jewish, he did his 23andMe. And here's a thing that is really taboo, that is really difficult to express publicly. Israelis and Palestinians, we are very similar in our DNA. Because these peoples were sharing space for centuries. And yes, you've seen the infographics that it was eighty percent Palestinian on the landmass between the river and the sea, there weren't even that many Jews in the area. We've all seen all these infographics. Genetically, biologically, and culturally though, we are very, very similar, in fact, and there is a much longer history of Jewish people and Arabs, Muslims, and also specifically Jews and Palestinians, living in the same places than there is a history of slaughter, apartheid, and forced displacement.

War is . . . an insane reality. It is like an insanity that seems to infect and affect everything. As we get sucked into the mind of war, it seems to make all kinds of other evil possible. This mind—it seems to perpetuate and to bring about all kinds of other evil that isn't even really about the war itself. It almost feels like a mind virus. A virus that eats hearts and brains.

I haven't even said a word, for example, about Ukraine. I haven't even said a word, for example, about Sudan, or Syria. Because we don't have a live feed of those conflicts. Or because I don't feel ancestrally shamed—personally shamed—by them.

But I remember when Putin invaded Ukraine, I remember I couldn't sleep for a month. And I'm talking to you now because I trust you guys. And because we have a shared history of studying and thinking and feeling together. I'm haunted by certain images of these beautiful human beings that are suffering for reasons that are completely man-made, and totally unnecessary.

And I'm also holding in my consciousness, and in my being, the people whose faces I have not seen, the people whose faces I cannot see . . .

I was raped when I was twenty. I was broke in Paris and a painter did it.

I just kind of put that experience away, but I didn't realize how it fermented in my body

Til something happened at a university.

There had been times a boyfriend would choke or hit me

Or throw me on the ground.

I didn't really understand—me. I felt I needed external

Force to make my heart beat. It was hard to write a sentence.

I had a somewhat meaningful poetry career, touring the world with a face encased in carbuncular boils, never having any money, while my mother lived with my brother in a dilapidated apartment lined with black mold, which she eventually got evicted from, and then I gave her my place.

People fell in love with me even though I bled from my face onto their faces while we made love and rose from a pillow stained with makeup.

I hid in the day and I hid in the dark and even under the darkness, boiling, in hiding I remained.

Your body is something you can force to move, like a disembodied mind controlling a robot from afar. The most terrible relationship—you parade your avatar into the world like a drone operator and—look at it suffering! You behold it dispassionately, like a scientist with no heart.

My soul kept pushing through and throwing its protest into my guts and splattering my face with its shrapnel.

I felt distended, like a traveler's bag loaded down with heirlooms it could not possibly be expected to keep from breaking, let alone carry safely into the promised land.

In the dark some kind of beauty emanated from me, apparently. In the dark I was told I looked like Ancient Greece, Puerto Rico, Andalucia, a goddess. And so on. In the dark the edge of beauty around which my demons slavered appeared on occasion to my lovers to be a whole country.

After I broke up with a particularly beautiful boyfriend I remember sobbing "I am tired of being an ugly Jew" to a friend who understood what I meant.

Even now as I type these words I am not entirely certain what I meant.

Nothing I learned at the university equipped me to deal spiritually or practically with the violence I had known—without me or within me.

Nothing I was taught prepared me for mystical visions either.

I was taught nothing about healing.

I was marked out for ugliness and difference from a young age and for a period of time I was able to draw energy and power from the complete impossibility and total torture of my position.

Theory existed about the monstrous and about horror. I didn't read much of it, but people who read my books often referred to it. Kristeva in particular, but others also.

My inner feeling was somewhat more fragile and hopeful. I had an idea I could somehow protect my soul from meaninglessness if I could write.

The problem with writing was I had been forced into it.

I was driven into literature. I was shoved into it.
I'd been attracted to it, yes, I had noticed it. But I was attracted to many things.

I was driven into literature with horrible force and what shocked me when I found myself there, inside of it, was that it was something alive.

It was not dead at all. It was a world that was living and completely capable of receiving me.

I was a sophomore at Barnard in my spring semester when my mother first became homeless. My grandfather had died on Y2K, when the world had been supposed to end.

I remember Britney Spears played Times Square that year. I didn't go to see the ball drop but my little brother had had a nervous breakdown and I remember walking through Times Square with him after midnight and taking him out for cake and soda around two a.m.

I offer these details to stand in for an ocean of other details. I gave myself very little time to write this book. I gave myself only enough time to come up to the very edge of the violence and shame I have known within myself.

It is immensely gratifying to me to write these terrible words.

I tore love and beauty from the world under those conditions, and stole from it my meager supper. I made my way around the culture, showing up when and where I was invited.

That's been one of the graces of my life. I have always been outside and have yet to figure out the meaning of home or belonging. But there's always been someone inviting me.

People are lovely and their loveliness humiliates my inner rage against myself. It has softened me and sometimes confused me. Gradually I have softened too. Then I came to miss the fearless, hideous girl. The one who first threw herself at beauty. The one who was hurled into literature violently, and who ransacked it desperately. Looking for an antidote . . .

*

Long sleep of ghouls and demons.

Last night was warm and stormy. I wrote things down that aren't true—but they are.

I dreamed of a stairway that led to a fine hotel that I had seen before. Kind of like the Spanish Steps in Rome.

Going up the stairs were men in complicated and tormented sexual arrangements, like visions of Hieronymus Bosch, but they were young and clean and well groomed, like Hilfiger and Abercrombie models.

Their faces—the look of concentration—showed a solemnity and an intensity one very seldom sees. Like in real life—you don't see such faces even in porn. You see it seldom and only on people who are utterly focused on a kind of devotion within their own suffering. They can't possibly know this shows on their faces. They are far from a place that would know what their own face looks like.

I have seen it sometimes on women in the gym. The orgiastic need for punishment.

But I don't see it often.

But I know it when I see it. I recognize something of myself in what I see: the yearning to give of myself totally, to take great pains to give totally. It is a look of great concentration. It isn't only torment. It is focus and concentration.

But it's a sick look: the worship of suffering.

It's also—the yearning to worship, but there's nothing to worship. So you worship your own suffering.

I have to repeat that I have seldom seen this face. You will sometimes see it in a lover. At times it shows on someone's sleeping face.

This time, these men on the stairs, and I should add that they were all clothed—khaki shorts and polo shirts—their legs spread wide, their arms held behind their back by other men, while other men set upon them—

It was a scene of extreme repression and sexual concentration to the point it was almost demonic. Crotches of khakis touching, and that spiky sebhorreic emanation of extreme emissions of testosterone and heat as you sometimes smell and feel them in gym environments, places where men's exertion and erotic desire is collectively charged to the point it becomes frightening, infinitely charged without release—the fume of their energy or just the energy of their energy felt noxious to me.

Like a poison coming out of their bodies.

I remember this from the dream. Their grunts, that they remained clothed, their bodies pinned in stress positions, all up and down the length of the stairs, the concentration of all the energy in their bodies into a concupiscent cruelty without release—

And when you got to the top you were met by the stone verandah of a fine hotel.

I booked a room. It was number 106 or 108. Something happened in there. A film was shown to me that was horrible—a horror film of some kind, but it was a documentary about a twentieth-century serial killer, projected against the wall. It was already playing when I got into the room the way TVs often are when you walk into a hotel room these days, and I couldn't find the remote control or button to turn it off.

There was a ghoulish man with shining tormented eyes who insisted on giving me a gel manicure. I felt guilty to judge him by his appearance.

The staff at the bar and front desk were polite, clean, and well groomed. They resembled the men on the stairs but without the hormones of sex charging their auras. They were breezy, bland, cool, solicitous, even friendly.

Yesterday I cried almost all day. I mean, I didn't cry all

day straight, but I cried many many times throughout the day and my eyes stayed wet and they kept opening.

In a way it's as though—I dreamed I refused to fight back against any injustice.

I dreamed of a world of aggression, pain, and achievement.

I dreamed of something devilish—repression and sexual torment.

Like a Tower of Babel. Like hell.

Somehow in the dream I was forced back into the room. And the murder film was shown to me again and I was forced to watch it. In the morning when it was over, incoherently I tried to tell the hotel staff what had happened, even though it was obvious they were running a hotel for this purpose and they were the same men tormenting themselves and each other on the stairs.

A reader whose purpose was to misunderstand me could easily detourn what I have described and say, That sounds like a great hotel. That sounds like a sexy place.

But how can I explain to you. It was a realm of demonic energy and devotion to pain. Not the "beautiful" suffering wherein our tears spit and cum water the Earth and world compassion emanates from our couplings.

It was a world of I and me and mine. It was SORT and FUCK and KILL.

It felt very real.

I still feel sick.

*

Yesterday I felt I was going to break again, that I can't live my life inside this culture. It was as bad as I felt in October and November, but worse because worse things have happened since then. And worse because I have been trying powerfully to concentrate. And meditate. And focus somehow on loving and repair.

It's not this year I first lost sleep over Palestine. It's been all my life. I lost sleep over my mother too and my grandmother, always, all my life.

Shame is a demon too. But if I didn't feel any shame whatsoever, if I knew in my heart and soul what people have been telling me since I was a child, that what happened to my mother wasn't my fault—who would I be? What and who would I be?

I *have* to blame myself.

Who but me myself will even ask me these questions? No one would drag me before the Grand Inquisitor. They will just bury my work and stop talking to me. Exile me from the family—as has already happened. Bury me completely. And steal from it when it suits them.

Who will interrogate my soul if not me? Who will recount the nightmares paraded before it? Who will document how my soul shuddered and guttered like a flame in torment to see so much evil done in this world?

Even if only a robot will read this.

If I were another person I would simply say, My name is Ariana and I stand against this evil.

But my name is Ariana and I feel no words exist for prophylaxis against it.

No words but that my soul must belong to this world as yours does, and if this evil is on me then it is on you too, you who claim to "stand" against it.

I fell in love with someone who fell in love with me. It's been years since I could love. I must be on the right path I thought. If I am able to love again. Not the path to success or even flourishing, but the next step beyond bare life, that to love must be the right and good—the natural outcome of all the agony and alienation I've been documenting . . .

*

Adrenaline floods your body when it is struck and in the

moment you feel no pain. It is intellectually exhilarating—almost like triumph. You reconnect to your heretofore obscured capacity for executive functioning.

You rejoice in your capacity to sort phenomena and prioritize rational action while your blood drips down onto the screen of your phone, and down your breast, and down your face.

Like the morning the mirror fell on me, the morning of my aunt Jeana's wedding.

I called my neighbor and she came over to remove the longest blades of glass from my hair and then she got in the shower with me and delicately picked tinier and tinier barbs from my skull, while I directed her movements to one portion and another of my wounds with the calm of an air traffic controller.

Then she drove me to the hospital where, from a gurney, I texted my assistant to cancel that morning's class.

They put six staples in my head.

For the next few weeks I read and reread Baudelaire's "L'Amour et le crâne"— "Love and the Skull," as it tends to be translated.

The poem describes a lamp in which a human skull is crowned by a Cupid figure, as though Love requires a kind of trepanation in order to retake dominion over the mind.

But I'm describing my own view of my injury *through* the prism of the poem, not analyzing the poem itself.

Somewhere in here is a parable—at least one—of violence.

I remember the whole week prior to the mirror falling on me I had been longing for physical punishment. The luteal phase of my cycle is often like this. It's not only my body that dilates and swells—it's reality itself, and all phenomena.

And my essential energy does not flow smoothly. It surges and ebbs, so that spatial and temporal relations swell and burst and become cloudy, like futurist and cubist paintings waving in and out of photorealism, wishful thinking, and intimations of catastrophe.

I remember writing down a craving for punishment and then I remember punishment arriving.

Needless to say I did not go to my aunt's wedding. I stayed home and watched seedpods float through the air in an uncommonly orgiastic springtime.

*

My aim had been to avoid memoir, but I need to describe some of the entanglement through which this effort— this book—arose.

It's a chronicle on some level of (my) pain, and an attempt

to disambiguate one family's suffering from the story of a whole people; to reckon out the limits of "personal healing" where it makes an X with "state violence." With war.

To write that one has always been against war is essentially meaningless at this point, but I'm a poet and it does bear writing such a sentence and explaining it.

9/11 took place on the first day of my senior year of college. I protested the then-impending War on Terror on the streets of New York and Washington D.C.; then I left the country. I protested the Global War on Terror in Paris. I thought I would become an exilic writer as it had been done in the twentieth century.

All of my books have entered the English language through its destruction and manipulation by war, first through the malapropisms of John Ashcroft and George W. Bush and then through the vogue for English's self-deadening in the I-and-me-oriented language of blogs and social media.

Can one "be" against war in one's body while wholly bound up in complicity with it?

While using its language?

While using its language against oneself?

Can one be "against" war while sober about the procedures of statecraft and realpolitik, without merely proclaiming oneself a pacifist, as if one lived in a vacuum, or a religious zealot, or a coddled intellectual skilled in the weaponization of extreme language while living a life of bourgeois comfort?

Can one accuse one's friends of failing to "speak out" and "use their voices" in a rotted public where robots are trained on your every word and gesture?

Can one understand war and borders, as Bataille did in *The Accursed Share*, as an expenditure of excess, a formalized mass ritual in erotics wherein the tensions between peoples and the friction between cultures might stimulate vitality even as they also lead to conflagration, catastrophe, and death?

I'm looking for something I can use . . .

Having to do with my own internalized violence and a self-abnegatory inheritance. A belief I somehow assimilated that certain people deserve to suffer forever and that I was one such person.

A kind of inner condescension to a feminine yearning in me that war must come to an end, that it has never worked, and that *both* the Empire and the Resistance are viciously cruel and depraved when it comes to women and children, whom "we" always purport to be protecting.

It's been war my whole life.

The Holocaust didn't properly end for me, or I stayed too close to it, because my mother was proof it hadn't ended. Her body fell onto mine when the War on Terror started.

She invaded my life.

"Who is responsible for the suffering of your mother?" asks Bhanu Kapil in *The Vertical Interrogation of Strangers*.

Live with this question and you'll realize it isn't a simple one to answer. It becomes almost mantric in its demands and in what it leads to.

My father is responsible for my mother's suffering. Hitler is responsible. The slaughter of my grandmother's family describes the shape of my mother's suffering. Israel is responsible. The peasants of Poland, the dybbuk in my grandmother's body. Judaism, smashed to smithereens, is why my mother suffered. I also am at fault. I was angry at her almost immediately.

The first sentences I ever wrote—ever in my life—were sentences against her. You'll see. I will tell you.

The couple-form in twentieth-century heterosexuality, psychiatry, late capitalism, the immigrant experience. Inherited trauma, spiritual homelessness, dread of the state. The limits of science. Survivor's guilt. The murder of god. Materialism. They are responsible for the suffering of my mother.

Her desire to rescue her parents from their suffering, to make her existence the antidote to their suffering—but also, her envy of their pain, which swallowed everything—this dynamic is perhaps the crux of her madness. The war was over, but not for her. She stayed inside it and so therefore did I.

Nonviolence is no longer respected among the intellectuals I know. It is seen to play into neoliberal and colonial aims. It is seen as soft.

Femininity as I've gradually grown into it—I always yearned for it—has become for me the dynamic through which I wrestle with my own violence and consciously decide to do something different with it than attack outwardly.

Inner violence as I have known it becomes a vector of auto-fertilization and a mode of transmutation.

It is also something that I indulge. Something bad for me. That I do anyway. A forbidden lust that at times I have watched make me very very ugly.

Nonviolence is no longer a strategy "we" respect. I am not yet at the point of being able to practice nonviolence inwardly.

But if I am honest, nonviolence is a strategy *I* respect. Because I find it tremendously difficult.

For it is true what they say on Instagram: In this age you have to love yourself. You must. It is imperative, and comes easier to some than others.

It may be that my rage against myself has been a product of state cruelty, the successful concatenation of the many corporate and state pressures that would deprive me of my own mind and body, of my own flourishing.

I know that I had every right to be angry. My father abandoned my mother and she went insane and when I was still a teenager she became my responsibility.

I hated him for that but I hated her too. I resembled her and I fled this resemblance. I was not a good daughter. I was close to self-murder and I feel lucky that I never went so far as to physically harm her or myself. I loved her like a husband—the kind of husband who would divorce her and take her children. I loved her like a father—the kind of father who would blame her for not turning out the way he wanted.

I comprehended the loathing of all softness. It lived in me. But I loved it too—the way you could love a forest that you yourself had burned down. The way Saint Julian would come to love every animal he had killed.

January 11, 2024—Invisible College

This is an experiment.

I'm looking at a surfer crashing into the waves, in a deserted, almost deserted beach town.

I hope you can hear the waves.

My phone is very low on space and on battery.

I wanted to try to send out a meditation for this New Moon in Capricorn Day, January 11, 2024.

When I first met Michel André and we sat down together in 2010, I was in Haiti being a relief worker.

I had always carried in my heart and in my mind the figure of an instructor, of a teacher, of a father, of a rabbinical figure, of an authority that I could actually believe in, as such. But I had never encountered such a person.

I longed for a teacher so much that I couldn't even say it out loud.

In other words, I went to Haiti in 2010 ostensibly as a relief worker, but really, it was a spiritual pilgrimage. I went in search of a teacher but it was such a taboo to admit—even to myself—that I wanted or needed a teacher, that I didn't say it out loud until he appeared.

Such figures are required in this world. We cannot have only corrupted authorities.

It creates an internal sickness, especially when you are young and somehow outside of everything.

There's a deep human need to hold high—to give honor—to also give and receive trust.

When I was younger—and this was maybe partly my own sensibility—but what was respected intellectually, at university, was the most extreme and the most insane forms of expression—whether in writing, in philosophy, or in art. Likewise riots and revolution.

It was an aesthetics of madness. Insanity was affirmed as a legitimate response to an insane society. And in many ways I *get* this. After all, my own mother was insane.

But it was Susan Sontag—I don't remember if she was talking about Artaud or Simone Weil—I remember reading a sentence of hers affirming the importance of sanity—and I worshipped Artaud and Simone Weil—and I remember thinking, What a lame-ass boring thing to say.

When I read that, I thought, Whatever, you're a bourgeois frump. Insanity is the only purity.

Typical young poet attitude.

I have since thought about it so much over the years and actually Susan Sontag was right. Weil and Artaud are important, but sanity is also extremely important and its value needs to be affirmed.

It seems important to connect this—the balance of sanity and insanity—to The Fool in the Tarot.

The Fool was how I could dare go to Haiti. The Fool is the poet card, and it's thanks to foolishness I have gradually been able to untie the knot of my own family, history, destiny.

As artists we all have this great privilege—even a responsibility—to untie ourselves from the noose of everything we come from and to go into the world making meaning anew.

I am speaking about a realm beyond good and bad, right and wrong, a foolish realm of play. I am not speaking about justice, I am not speaking about slaughter or war, or the oppressed becoming oppressor. I can't speak to any of those things today—

I'm trying to correlate a fool's errand, a foolish life, a fool's ontology to the law of real authority, a kind of leadership and prestige and power that you can actually respect and that you can wholeheartedly honor because it is legitimate, legitimate and worthy power that is sane, that is not insane, that would put fair and also gentle and understanding limits on the infinite, not to be lame and frumpy and bourgeois and boring, but to make it possible for something to take root and for growth to happen . . .

The psychological is maybe always a little bit more boring than the mystical.

When this war started I wrote something and I was praying, I prayed, Please, God, don't let me become a hypocrite. I don't even really know what I meant. I think it had to do with deadening and cutting off parts of my soul in order to withstand the moment.

States, governments, countries bordered by hostile entities, all of those political machinations are real, and I don't think, in fact I know, it's not for my—for many of our—lack of human compassion—it's not for lack of intelligence or care for human life or care for Palestinians that this war has not yet ended. The sorrow and shame over it has been collectivized while the powerful do what they do and profit from it. It's almost like the financial collapse of 2008, when the entire country was made to pay for the evil actions of a few, who were propped up and supported, and who our outrage and misery disturbed not one iota. This war on Palestine, it feels like it is exploiting deeply corrupt and decayed structures that have locked themselves together in opposition, completely fastened to each other, and that through this decay a huge amount of blood is pouring . . . and they don't care about this blood. It does not seem to disturb them.

There's brilliant strategy and cruelly cynical genius on display in this world. How can it not horrify us, how can we not want it to stop.

I wonder if I am about to say a sick thing. There's a way in which this horror pouring into the world also feels like a horrible—horrific—counterweight to, or maybe actually consequence of, the mechanistic—machine-like—forces that are also moving across the world and through hearts and bodies and consciousness.

I'm talking about the dread of the apocalypse of machines they've been selling us.

This idea that animal life, human life, is somehow inferior to the machine mind that is in the process of learning. A kind of Frankenstein god in its uncontrollable infancy . . .

Our technocrats are obsessed with the idea we will be subjugated by superior machines. They have slave minds.

I feel that we're being asked this year, at this time when so much is collapsing, so much feels emotionally, socially, and practically ridiculous or unbearable, when meaning itself, which has been being fucked with my whole adult life—

We're being asked to live fully in the paradoxical and contrasting states in which we find ourselves, to live into—deeply into—very extreme contradictions in being, and intellect, and somehow stay focused on the prize of seeking love and goodness, of creativity.

Somehow your own consciousness must stay fully within the mystical timeline, while fully engaged in very practical acts and very practical action.

You could be welling up in tears one minute, and then you could be numb for days, or weeks, in one region of yourself, while another region of yourself remains fully warm, and fully alive to every particularity and sensitivity of a moment or a person, or an idea, or a project that you're working on.

I am not sure if this makes sense. It's as though we are being asked to remain fully alive while pouring our consciousness into different parts of ourselves while other parts rest.

I think the danger is to go completely numb, to become over-accustomed to compartmentalization, to become devoured by sadness or rage, or to become cynical and through your own cynicism to reproduce the cruelty you're seeing evidence of everywhere.

You have to attend to these paradoxes in the real and hold them all and develop your consciousness around this holding of them all.

This task correlates somewhat to Julian of Norwich beholding all the contradictions of vast creation in the palm of her hand, in a sphere the size of a hazelnut.

I am thinking also of an instruction from the Diamond Sutra: Develop a mind that abides nowhere.

I think this is part of the instruction of this moment, to reckon with these paradoxes of our culture and our own lives, and to develop the agility—we who have the privilege of not having bombs falling on our heads and not literally being the ones physically dropping them— to develop the agility to find something to respect, inside ourselves and outside ourselves, and to hold high. The diamond of the mind itself—in spite or irrespective of its atmosphere.

Because there's quantum reality existing at all times and pervading all times, at all time and every point of space. And that therefore means that holiness and wisdom are coexisting with all of this wretchedness. Our task is not to forget this, and to look for the wisdom and the medicine that is always available, even—maybe especially—at a time like this.

GRANADA

It was raining on the Alhambra
Just like I knew it would
But in my vision they let me in
While in reality they would not
So I took refuge in a Zara
With every other woman in Granada
Despite the well-deserved boycott
I was dirty from the plane
Wanted to see myself in large mirrors
And once I was a little drier
I went around the corner
& found a shop that sold the ink my pen needs
The airport is named after Lorca
Probably the moon belongs to him
Not only the moons of Andalucía
But every moon, everywhere
The Falangists shot him not too far from here
With pistols of silver, or so I've heard
The Sacred Heart of Jesus was his middle name
He was miserable in New York as a young man
I too was miserable there—Columbia—
Lorca described a city of wires destroying Black bodies
Slavering over his soul. He does have a way of making love
To his torment that sickens me. All poets
Are brothers. The rain makes me feel old
The color of walked-upon stones
James Fenimore Cooper walked here
And my grave, sunken-eyed ancestors
On my father's side, scholarly and swart

Here Ferdinand and Isabella set things up with Columbus
Here it all began—or ended. Here it all ended.
Second the Moors, first the Jews. Torture.
Grenadine. Expulsion. Conversion. America.
The Americas. A document signed at the Alhambra.
The twisting double helix dividing soul from spirit
And spirit from body and foot from land
Whose poem snakes up to the moon? Lorca
Gives way to Darwish. My stars take refuge in their beards
While I keep up my act of the idiot woman
She creates a diversion so we can keep up our studies
Underground. She ages hysterically where people can see
So that I can raise my children . . .

For Sasha Frere-Jones, 1/1/24

All I can think about is that for more than two months the heart of the entire world has been goaded to new heights by a genocide unfolding. It brings horror, insanity, numbness but also clarity, strategy, grave honesty.

My religion and the sufferings and triumphs of my family have been totally desecrated. Personal sorrow: that my family abandoned my mother and left her to my brother and me, that finally she killed herself, when the psychosis that protected her own soul from its pain finally gave way to reality. She hardly got out from under the Holocaust long enough to give birth to us before she went flipping insane.

Slogans, flags, the notion of the ownership of land—it all withers me, makes my heart shudder, makes me think of Hitler and the peaceful cows of Bavaria.

For me, Judaism and non-assimilation, non-Zionism—which is the same as nonviolence, at least in my own body—have translated to radical homelessness and a commitment to the poet's life. I stick out. I do not fit. The culture glances at strange angles off my lines and the ironies provoked by the way I live. This is the only way I have figured out how to build, how to love. It has happened gradually. It began when I renounced my father's love, and the natural yearning to please him.

I feel social pressure to channel my personal experience into political action but I fall back upon the contemplation of my own defects and those of my direct line: my father, cold and narcissistic and authoritarian—in the very image of all the grave Abrahamic fathers that came before him. I refuse to ask him for anything. I called and called my fucking reps. I will send them gruesome postcards today. I do believe in democracy, in the so-called American experiment but I suffer from a Judaic melancholy when it comes to crowds. Even crowds I share values with. Righteousness, piety—I try to be very very careful and move very very slowly when I feel them rising within me.

To paraphrase a line by Ghayath Almadhoun: The real problem with war is the people who survive it. To which I add the silent lines I always hear in my head when I hear him read the poem containing this line: Because we who survive grow up to be perverts, because we who survive get fucked up.

But to return to my own tradition, which has been perverted, twisted, mutilated and massacred by the actions of the Israeli state and the weapons my tax dollars pay for—as long as I've lived—we have our cruel fathers and I have mine—but there is also an unwritten history of feminine, Hasidic, insanity that I'm heir to.

The real tradition isn't written in our books. The real Judaism is hidden in women's bodies.

Tears sprang to my eyes as I wrote that last sentence. How dare I write such a thing.

I have been sick with shame and dazed with blood. I will be told that such feeling is unrevolutionary and that to give into it is bourgeois.

I have been searching for a way to speak accurately and protest accurately that does not masculinize me, that does not find me hardening my speech into the eroticized militancy of the noble freedom fighter. Was it the cruel bathos of America—assimilation with its norms—that made my family go cold? Was it genocide that made those of us who came after—and those of us who remained—attack each other—and ourselves? Or was it some soul-stain in Judeity itself—that neither assimilation into the polite norms of white Protestantism nor alienating religiosity, neither mystical nor financial achievement, neither comedy nor tragedy—could clear?

*

I've been listening to Jordi Savall's album *Les Voix humaines* on repeat.

Savall is a Catalan viola da gamba player, conductor, composer, and innovative scholar of Baroque music—and also a profound antifascist, down to his very cell. I've used his music in sculpture and performance projects. It fills the void that my father's hardness and coldness—and my rejection of his hardness and coldness—left in my life. Savall's interpretations of Bach, Marin Marais, Couperin, and so on—when he plays I can hear not only the triumphs of Reason but a profound experience of its nightmares, to paraphrase Goya.

For me Savall is an example of leadership, death, the paternal and masculine principle functioning properly—knowing its history and being honest about it. Fulfilling his role with flair—without erasing mystery, or tragedy.

In short, the sound he makes answers my yearning for a father I could respect.

We are Spanish, on my father's side. Jordi Savall has a daughter named Arianna, two Ns. The sound of his viola da gamba, for me, is the true sound of men.

Obviously I am against war. Obviously I am against the slaughter of Palestinians. The wounds of Zion have been in my heart and a physical problem for me, a matter of physical shame and personal shame—my entire life. What pulls me and pushes me toward the darker chambers of my heart—the deeper unknown—is what my grandmother did to herself, felt she had to do—in order to go on. To have a family. And likewise my mother.

Oh yeah, and then there's me, and whatever it was I was doing to myself in order to build a home in this culture, however tiny, for the things one hesitates even to admit to oneself.

Because the Christmas holiday is about birth, and the Christ's body is essentially the feminization of the male body—the suffering male body made generative, the bloody wound in his side the double of the womb—and the Christ story is a myth you have to live under, in America, whether you consent to it or not—so the best you can do is interpret it correctly, even if it's not your story—well, I give you *Les Voix humaines*. Human voices. Consoling, grave, pure, and true.

This record sounds like everything I want to do.

An anguish had been removed from my life that might have finally made something middle-class and dignified really possible for me, or so I remember thinking the first week of October.

I could actually choose for the first time what I wanted to do with my life. Learn to love in new ways, and abandon the personae limiting, or so it seemed to me, the way my work had theretofore been understood.

I believed in short that I was on a personal path of healing.

My mother had killed herself. My father had refused to come to her funeral. And nevertheless, on October 2, I found it in me to acknowledge his birthday. After decades of him ignoring mine. It's not easy to talk about something like this. To show him love in this way required immense inner effort.

I wasn't actually living anywhere at that time. I was in an airbnb in the town I'd moved to during the pandemic. Just being in that town was enough to conjure, for the purposes of my writing, enough sense of home that I could more or less trust my sense perceptions and intuitions.

I was finishing a book called *The Rose*, about a romance I'd had in that town that had led me to a curiosity about the relationship of magical powers to sex with the wrong people, and just why and how, more specifically, certain famous magicians had "lost" their magic.

The book is about the question of the erotic mistake.

But to return for a moment to the war in me, as I understood it at that time—

I had a mother who was incapable ever of blaming herself or even so much as considering her own role in the calamities that befell her.

One could say, therefore, that I have abjured blaming others for my problems and predicaments to an almost pathological degree.

I won't even blame capitalism, my peer group's favorite enemy, for the various things that are wrong with me and the many dynamics that horrify and consternate me about this world.

It's just that I have to beware the mechanisms by which a mind can so easily devour itself because I've watched it happen to the people I love most.

Paranoid schizophrenia feeds on the vulnerabilities in a personality: the points of being that have least been loved in a person. It begins to eat her from there.

It happens in culture too.

I am not saying that there is no enemy or that when it came down to it I would not fight for, kill, and die defending what I love. I might.

I am saying that I have taken a kind of monastic vow with respect to blaming and that my sanity has in many respects depended on this vow.

Let me put this another way. By blaming myself for everything, essentially, or reserving almost all of my aggression *for* myself I have managed to maintain a *kind* of sanity.

It has its limits of course.

And my internalization of the various fields of battle—literal, cultural, political, and so on—can also be correlated, I think, to the erosion of public institutions, the decline of public trust in journalism and politics, and to an ambient sense of generalized distrust and alienation, not only as they have been fomented in the last four years, but my entire adult life.

There were simply too many people to blame and too much personal grievance available to me for me to construct a personality and an ethos with any coherence whatsoever around those things—even with the liberties I won by becoming a poet. Blame and grievance made people in my family insane. Forcing strangers to appease and bear witness to my outrage and hurt would leave me at dangerous risk of insanity. It would put my relief into the hands of others.

Poetry as I understand it is an art so naked it almost doesn't exist.

Sophisticated practitioners can hide their personality defects from it. But poetry's nudity is what interests me. The feeling that I don't know—can't know—what it will lead to. It cuts to the quick.

It teaches me about what is already happening to me. It is not a package in which I would preserve a memory, or a system through which by showing you how misunderstood I am I can extract love from you.

I recognize the reality of a concatenation of criminality and cruelty that has mediated my attempts at liberty as a poet. There are people and institutions I am angry at. In fact I am filled with aggression. I simply cannot indulge in unleashing it on others. It leaks out sometimes, but mainly, I am the one I have the right to punish.

I want to be punished. I want to pay my debt to society inside me. And I want to be redeemed. And I want to be released.

When I agreed to go to Europe and do this tour I had only been writing poems again in a way that felt at all like me for a few months.

It was because I was playing tricks on myself that I'd been able to write again—but the tricks were working. And I remember thinking, I could build a new personality around this self-knowledge. That I don't need a literal home, but just its atmosphere, to devote myself to the nudity that obsesses me—to feel like I am making contact with my own soul not merely due to animal comfort or normal human needs, but this deeper need that haunts me when I can't figure out how to answer it.

Poets existed before writing, but without writing, I cannot shape my soul.

Inside me is an animal that needs certain things to feel familiar but also fresh and relatively without consequence in order to make meaning through my body in such a way it coheres.

In other words a kind of simplicity helps me reach inner places that are easily lost track of.

I wasn't thinking about myself psychologically at that time. My body read the world for me so I could write. It felt like the vector of a larger liberation: skills I had learned in agony now helped me hold the pen.

✽

I kept having the sense, over and over especially those last few years, that I was always on the verge of losing my soul, that my mind was being fought for and eroded, my powers of creation and my autonomy of thought—like if the culture itself didn't devour me my family would.

But there was also the part that was my responsibility. Immense rage.

I would periodically regain territory within myself and be flooded, as it were, with lucidity or vision, occasionally also an entrepreneurial spirit. Then something would happen. A change of circumstance. Something catastrophic, or sudden love. I would have "learned something about myself." I would make a consequential mistake or stop myself from making it. I would hold myself apart from people, or I would fall back in with them.

It was sort of like meditating in a casino, or writing your thesis in airports and bus stations. Both of which in fact I had done.

In a way every book I've written is about the dread of engulfment. Jonah's anatomy of the whale.

There was a need for home and familiarity and certainly a need for therapy when my mother died, but I had no home and I hadn't been able to figure out a doctor either.

It was maybe because of something that had changed in my mind one night in LA, when I was still living there, and how that change shifted how I came to relate to older forms of anguish that by then I had built many habits around.

*

When my mother killed herself I had happened to be in New York. Everything about my mother's death was englobed in a kind of perfection and that perfection even held my weeping. I want to tell you about how it happened but not because I desire your sympathy.

I simply want you to understand that I had been marked out to live the life of a woman with problems, and that every book I had written while my mother was alive was conscious of this curse without going so far as to literally spell it out.

Her death was the surgical removal of my one and only real problem: Everything else was negotiable.

I could pull myself together now.

I could change.

You pray every day and work every day for the removal of your curse and when it is finally taken away, who are you? Who do you become?

How many generations after enslavement does it take the people to comprehend liberty. What does it mean to be born free and not to know it.

I was just beginning to emerge from my curse when the new war started.

Definitely the way I was handling money and not dealing with the basic need for home were signs that I was suffering—throwing my life away in ways I had learned to do all my life: for art.

But the floating was soothing. And *The Rose* kept me focused. *The Rose* was what I trusted to lead me to the next place.

I came "home" form LA to the town I'd lived in during the pandemic. I pretended to be "home" in its cheaper airbnbs.

There was a corner behind the parking lot of the courthouse that I loved, where my favorite trees had grown and then been chopped down. I was familiar with the morning light, the coffee places, the bars, and a few of the people. There was one person I'd slept with under bad circumstances whom I tried to avoid and a couple of people with weird energy, a new raft of city people who didn't know how to return a small-town smile—I remember a woman folding herself back into the doorframe of her building once, like she was stuffing an envelope and sealing it—completely canceling the impulse to step outside with her golden retriever—because she could not pull herself together to return my smile.

It was raining that day and I was about to start teaching *Paradise Lost*. The war hadn't started yet. Red apples were nodding in the trees. An AI had stolen a book of mine, and books by many of my friends. The feeling that week was that what was coming was something digital and cold that would separate us from the passions and intensities that had driven us into art in the first place—

That "AI" was somehow "coming." That a force was rising to challenge and devour the artifacts of the human soul, and the soul's reality.

It was the Promethean spirit I had wanted to study when I first resolved to study Milton.

A computery feeling hovered behind the moneyed derangement of the city people walking up and down the one walking street in my town, single-origin espressos in hand, pretending not to see me.

I thought I was beginning to feel and see how to finally consciously build a life. What I was trying to prepare myself for spiritually was to stay human in the face of the computer.

I tried to release my rage against my father. Five days later it was October 7.

Plunged into hell. Into a Jewish hell, which we don't believe in.

The computer was where the killing took place, for us, and the computer did a lot of the sorting and the killing, also.

I remember throwing myself into the emptiness of poetry. I stopped sleeping.

I studied the war and its history. All of us did. I read everything about it, books and essays, I took in everything "both sides" were saying. All sides. I studied the war constantly, hours into the night, and I surveilled myself.

I wrote letter after letter to a network of progressive media Jews I'm part of. I thought we could stop the war. I thought the American left could unite with the Israeli left and we could stop it. I felt personally implicated and disgusted by it. Already I had always felt personally implicated and disgusted by the Occupation—by "always" I mean since my late teens.

But I also questioned myself. I questioned my worship of leftist revolution and my cultural inheritance in the literature of transgression. Maybe I was a simpleton after all. Maybe I didn't understand what is really at stake in geopolitics. Maybe I would have been happier had my family emigrated to Israel. Maybe I would have been less alienated and had better self-esteem.

One friend texted me relentlessly during the first few weeks of the slaughter. She had worked for the Red

Crescent in Ramallah. We will never ever live this down, she said. "We" meaning Jews.

I imagined Judaism itself being swallowed into the earth. And I sobbed a very strange kind of tears—tears I had never shed in my life. Tears of sympathy and bitter regret for Israel, a country I had always loathed, even to the faces of my Israeli friends. I was crying, I realized, for a place my mother and grandmother had loved.

I missed my mother and grandmother.

I longed for their happiness, the memory of which I retained only a few fragments, from when I was a little girl. My mother had picked apples on a kibbutz and slept soundly at night to machine gun fire from Lebanon. She said she was never afraid, and the apples were the most delicious she had ever tasted. For my grandmother, as for most Holocaust survivors, Israel meant "never again." I had argued with her over it as a teen and finally felt sorry for it.

But I need to be precise about a few things. October 7 did not elicit sympathy for Israel from me—whether because I had been primed to hate the "Zionist Oppressor" by a lifetime in experimental poetry or internalized racism I am not sure. I started crying for it when the retaliation started. I was crying for my entire bloodline. I was ashamed but also tormented, and I wished that I had ever been able to love myself Jewishly as fully as others seemed to be able to. To love myself enough to defend myself, for example.

Of course I preferred Kafka to Bernie Madoff. And I hated my father.

It was a confusion in me. I took the bait. I became angry at Judaism itself, not merely Israel. I felt cursed. Then I tried to separate the Jewish state from Judaism, and would succeed for a day or two, before succumbing again. Israel was my father. But I felt alienated from so many progressive Jews too. At this point I was more of a witch—completely Jewish, but disabused of some of Judaism's self-entitlements thanks to my miserable family, and the rest exfoliated by my misadventures in poetry.

✳

I tried to reject the mechanisms of blame. Balfour, Hamas, Hitler, Ferdinand and Isabella. I tried to practice a constant meditation on nonduality. I was scared of becoming the war.

At the same time, I could not stop punishing myself. This was something left over from when my mother was alive.

I didn't want to surrender my body to politics. I was scared to let go of my mother and put my body in a crowd. I was scared to become a host body for an agenda, a lobby, a social sickness, for anything.

I decided I would only blame myself.

You may be thinking: To reject the mechanisms of blame (except of myself) and to renounce public moralizing—is cowardice. That to turn inward in the ways I have described—in times like these—is unheroic and unrevolutionary.

I think this is true. I am only heroic and revolutionary within myself. The space of the social and the collective, the space of institutions and of the state—I don't trust them.

I could not give up my grief so fast. It took me too long to let go of my family—even after I rejected them, even after they started to die.

To reserve the right to self-punishment is also to detourn the power of social censure and political repression—to refuse to be their subjects.

It is also a way of saying: Only I have the right to punish me.

Notice the distinction. I am not denying the need for discipline and punishment.

To make someone pay—to make me pay—for all this evil.

But it's given my life meaning.

Poetry is a naked artform that comes from inside you but also from all around you.

You can do poetry with absolutely nothing, and I have.

The artform has a peculiar relationship to poverty and the history of poverty among artists. The discipline's major practitioners, especially of the twentieth century, especially in and around New York, were explicitly not interested in money.

The wealth was in your responsibility and even better your right to know everything poets have ever known and to create through the known lineages existing in all poetries of the planet through all time—to create with absolute freedom earned by the living reality that anyone could be a poet and you had elected yourself as such.

Maybe it's because I was being taught by a poet of the New York School when my mother first became homeless. A kind of immensity of spirit had become terribly compressed—crushed even, by circumstance—and the conditions of this crushedness had become the green fuse driving the flower, as it were—like my work had to be provoked by extreme pain and essentially, impossibility.

It kept flowering into the impossible and whatever life was or opportunities, they pulled me forward through that void.

Today I drew The Ace of Swords.

The sword is cognate to the spade and to the pen. The toil of Cain and the violence of the word.

Then a poet I met by accident in 2016, when my then-partner and I were living a life of pilgrimage, sent me four photographs she took of us in the famous watermelon-hued dining room in Stonington, Connecticut, where James Merrill and David Jackson first began their experiments with the Ouija board in 1955, the experiments that would lead to a poem I'm preparing to teach, *The Changing Light at Sandover*.

"Walls of a ready-mixed matte 'flame' (a witty/ Shade, now watermelon, now sunburn)" is how Merrill describes that dining room in the poem.

I've had experiences of its prophetic accuracy that lead me to sense the poem itself is alively aware of what the watermelon has come to mean.

I looked at the photos sent to me by the poet on my phone just now, but it hurt to see what I looked like at that time.

It was like being gnawed by a boar to see how I was then. At the time living also felt fanged as my face often was. It was as though my inner organs also had knives and teeth.

I was angry inside and I didn't know how to stop it.

I will have to leave aside the charged space of poetic mediumship for now—because I want to talk about how ugly I feel I look in the photographs I just received, and by "ugly" I suppose I mean that I see pain in these pictures I was completely incapable of hiding.

I was trying to move it, I was trying to transmute it . . . I swear to you that I was trying.

I look cubist—like every part of my body is angry at the center—it's a soul throwing up spikes and decoys against the light of reality—I resemble someone who cannot make herself cohere to the world without a vigorous internal and practical effort.

I was hacking away at myself—I would have cut things off and moved them around, inflated here and shrunken there, if I could have afforded it then. I would have gone into witness protection.

I had just started meditating, my mother was about to become homeless again, I had torn the menisci in both knees in a performance at the Whitney Museum and somehow these torn menisci would effloresce with the vascular system in my legs when I was under stress and suddenly I'd lost the ability to bend my knees or walk at all.

I don't think any of the blood can have been moving correctly through my body.

It was about a year since the sun talked to me.

I knew I was going to lose my apartment. My partner and I, smiling together in James Merrill and David Jackson's dining room, were soon to lose each other. My mother was about to be on the streets again.

"Things" had grown dislodged and detached from their center inside me. I was burying "things" in various parts of my body.

The only "thing" I had right was when it happened from time to time that a poem saw me. And I moved my body accordingly.

The gender center between my love and me had become confused and our sex had stopped making sense.

My hair, a rug of curls, falls over a parched white face whose mouth folds in on itself, baring ratlike teeth. As if the flesh were trying to crawl back into the skeleton.

✱

Immense violence is in me. My ruler is Mars, the God of War. I always hated my father—I wanted to kill him even when I was a very little girl.

The first full sentences I ever wrote, I wrote to my mother—whom I adored.

I wrote that I hated her and that I wanted to kill her.

I could tell you the context to make you trust me more—
I could tell you that I'd been going to a one-room school-
house and playing with older kids at recess, that I'd
made friends with two older boys at the tire swing one
afternoon, and that, hearing them commiserate on how
much they hated their mothers—I realized I didn't hate
mine.

But I went home and wrote her the first letter I'd ever
write in my life and I told her that I hated her and that I
wanted to kill her.

I have no memory of liking those boys in particular or of
wanting to be liked by them. I only remember this act of
violence I committed against my mother with words, and
that she cried.

※

Where did it come from, this deep sense of ugliness that
still wells up in me? The sense of being stained and evil
and completely unworthy of life? What is the point of a
mouth full of knives, and the terrible sword?

Whenever I don't talk right my lip shape changes. When
I stop speaking I get rashes and eczema near my mouth.
It doesn't even take lying for this to happen to me—even
just silence is enough to afflict me.

What's the point of my existence as a Jew?

To live on the sword, so say the Zionists. The Hamas flag has a sword on it too. My sword points inward and I know my killer well.

The violence over which I have potential direct control: the violence in me.

Once upon a time, when I grew tired of this feeling of ugliness, I realized I could pray for beauty—nobody had to know.

I began lighting orange and yellow candles and filtering my water. The texture of my skin and hair began to change.

I had had a very beautiful lover. He was so beautiful I began to feel like a man. All the adoration in me had gone out of my body. It was as though my womanhood itself forsook me—I was working so hard in those days. I was working so hard that I also had to put in extra work to *resemble* a woman. I was so skinny and sick. I think my soul had left my body.

I've written about knives and swords for artists—because the cut-up was an influential technique and because every religious tradition will also speak of swords and blades in its way, when the time comes.

If I was going to be a blade I realized it was going to take a lot of practice not to become corroded by my own mettle.

I am sorry for that pun—in general I dislike them—but in this case it had to be done.

This photograph I am looking at shows two queer poets in their motley, in the famous Merrill–Jackson dining room.

I was in danger that afternoon and at that time in my life of turning totally into the bug and the rat of my own existence—its scavenger and its mere survivor.

I was so angry at my mother and father. I wanted to be a woman poet and I didn't know how.

I had been to Haiti and back four times.

I had been raped and my mother by then had told me that my father had raped her.

Which—I will never know if it was true.

I would take pills to make my heart beat. I only trusted literature.

I believed I could one day become good.

If I kept on trying to say yes—to reality.

The sword was me—I was the problem.

Absolute will and absolute rage—the daggers of the mind—all you have to do is look at my face and body in this photograph.

I was angry at nature. I did not trust myself. I knew nothing about women.

But I wanted to become one.

There may yet come a time when people no longer dig into their souls like this—not with a spade, not with a blade, and without the hope even a single other person may benefit from such labor.

Maybe we will change our souls cosmetically, or discipline them the way we do our bodies. Maybe we will all learn alchemy, and the terrible dysphoria we feel will be remedied at last from within.

March 19, 2024—Invisible College

The heart must open. And practice with this has to be undertaken by artists.

The works of art that we see nowadays, that are pervaded by a consciousness that is not incoherent or reactive are relatively few.

We make a mistake I think when we focus our energy on denouncing and pulling down, and a libidinal investment in heaping our disgust on everything that is so wrong, and I am not denying the wrongness.

The way the future has always come is people start building it before the bad stuff is over. One has to divest from dystopia, one has to divest from the libidinal surge of righteous superiority.

We all feel it and we all experience the need to separate ourselves somehow (even if only internally) from the kind of moral destitution, the viciousness mindlessness soullessness we see everywhere—but it has to be done without ourselves turning into the very thing we hate.

It takes active energetic curious engagement on a granular basis, vital energetic engagement even when sleeping, seven-days-a-week consciousness practice. To the degree to which poetry interests me, it interests me because of this: It has been a medium through which certain insights about the way things really are have come and do come . . .

Things come through poetry that help the world, instruct the soul, mend the heart.

The iron is hot right now. Standards for judgment, the old value systems by which we used to judge art works, cultural artifacts, even right and wrong action, all of that is up for review.

This is a time on the planet that we are shifting into a completely new era. New norms will solidify but they have not yet. It is exciting to get in there and work with this hot ore while it's hot, rather than waiting for it to cool, or waiting for someone else to shape it for you, because they will, whoever the powerful are, however they get it, if their influence over you is conceptual, linguistic or their literal boot in your face—they will shape what is to come for us, on top of us and against us, if we don't shape it for ourselves.

Dressed as a puritan

She picked a lemon off the ground

Green on one side

As the early womb

Wrapped in cloud

Was accused of having been full

Of fire. Two halves

Of the root of all things

Are touching in a lewd

& unstoppable way—leaking

Organ-pink light

More life than we know what to do with

ACKNOWLEDGMENTS

Thank you Marija Cetinić for invitations and gracious introductions at the Sandberg Institute and Perdu in Amsterdam and for organizing the tour that prompted me to write this book. Thank you Chloe Chignell and Sven Dehens at rile* Books in Brussels, Stefa Govaart for hosting me in conversation, and Nathalie Rozanes for first introductions. Thank you Bill Martin, Ghayath Almadhoun, Siddhartha Locknani, Erin Honeycutt, and everyone at Hopscotch Reading Room in Berlin. Thank you After 8 Books and Antonia Carrara and Rachel Valinsky for hosting me in conversation in Paris. Thank you *Mars Review of Books* for bringing me to Lisbon. Thank you björnsonova / Good Night Readers for bringing me to Prague.

"ABSOLUTE ZERO" was first exhibited at the Louvre in the exhibition *100 poètes du Louvre* in March 2024, curated by Donatien Grau, with a companion publication, *At the Louvre*, from NYRB Poets, and was also published by *Forever Magazine* in 2024. "DISINHIBITOR" first appeared in *The New Yorker* in December 2023. "THE FRONTIER" was written for Mai Thu Perret in April 2024.

With immense gratitude to Invisible College, and to my friends: I owe you my life.

Ariana Reines is a poet, playwright, and performing artist from Salem, Massachusetts and based in New York. Her books include *A Sand Book*—winner of the 2020 Kingsley Tufts Award and longlisted for the National Book Award—*Mercury*, *Coeur de Lion*, and *The Cow*, which won the Alberta Prize from Fence in 2006. Her Obie-winning play *Telephone* was commissioned by the Foundry Theatre with a sold-out run at the Cherry Lane Theatre in 2009. Reines has created performances for the Solomon R. Guggenheim Museum, the Swiss Institute, Stuart Shave/Modern Art, Le Mouvement Biel/Bienne, the Whitney Museum of American Art, and Performance Space New York. She has taught poetry at UC Berkeley (Holloway Poet), Columbia, NYU, and Scripps College (Mary Routt Chair), been a visiting critic at Yale School of Art, and for community organizations including the Poetry Project and Poets House. Her poetry and prose have been published in *The New Yorker*, *Poetry*, *Artforum*, *Frieze*, *Harper's*, and many others. In 2020, while a Divinity student at Harvard, Reines created Invisible College, an online space devoted to the study of poetry, sacred texts, and the arts.

Other books out with Divided

Night Philosophy by Fanny Howe
Fanny Howe walks with the prophets and with the unborn. There is no writer like her. —Ariana Reines

**In Pursuit of Revolutionary Love:
Precarity, Power, Communities** by Joy James
Joy James's Revolutionary Love is umph-degree love; or love beyond measure ... It is love that dares all things, beyond which others may find the spirit-force to survive. —Mumia Abu-Jamal

Disorganisation & Sex by Jamieson Webster
Who knew the hole was what Freud had in mind when he invented psychoanalysis and wouldn't stop saying 'sex'. Take a tumble into Wonderland with Dr Webster and decide for yourself what counts as real.
—Courtney Love

Bosses by Ghislaine Leung
Few artists dig deep into themselves like this: an extraordinary insight into the process of producing art.
—Cosey Fanni Tutti

Self-portrait by Carla Lonzi
Translated by Allison Grimaldi Donahue
As visual artists experimented with material, Lonzi experimented with human relations and their most mineral communications, gleaning their depths for a more radical subjectivity. —Quinn Latimer

Stage of Recovery by Georgia Sagri
Sagri's is an extraordinary example of a practice where, as with the Situationists, art becomes indiscernible from politics. —Mehdi Belhaj Kacem